TWO-HANDED TENNIS

Two-Handed Tennis

STRATEGIES TO INCREASE YOUR POWER, YOUR CONTROL AND YOUR SHOT-MAKING ABILITY

Jeffrey F. McCullough

Photographs by Cheryl Traendly

Foreword by Kathy Rinaldi

M Evans

Lanham • New York • Boulder • Toronto • Plymouth, UK

M Evans
An imprint of Rowman & Littlefield
4501 Forbes Boulevard, Suite 200
Lanham, Maryland 20706
www.rowman.com

10 Thornbury Road, Plymouth PL6 7PP
United Kingdom

Library of Congress Cataloging in Publication Data

McCullough, Jeffrey.
   Two-Handed tennis.

   Includes index.
   1. Tennis—Two-handed strokes.   I. Title.
GV1002.9.T86M33   1984   796.342'2   83-20759

ISBN 978-0-87131-491-8

Distributed by
NATIONAL BOOK NETWORK

Design by James L. McGuire

Manufactured in the United States of America

CONTENTS

FOREWORD

I first became interested in tennis—and two-handed tennis in particular—when I was eight years old. At that time, in the early 1970s, another young two-handed player from Florida, Chris Evert Lloyd, was beginning to make her mark on the tennis world. I still greatly admire Chris and, like so many others, give her a lot of credit for inspiring me to develop a two-handed backhand of my own.

There was never much doubt that I would become a two-handed player. When one is as young as I was when I began, it is very difficult to hit a good backhand with one hand. Like many other young players I knew and competed against, I was able to learn only the essentials of two-handed stroke production. I wish I had had a copy of *Two-Handed Tennis* to refer to back then. Young players taking up the game today will benefit greatly from the experience and insight presented by Jeffrey McCullough from his years of teaching two-handed strokes.

Of course, *Two-Handed Tennis* is not directed exclusively to children or beginners. More advanced two-handers, from club players to pros such as myself, can also gain valuable information about their individual styles of play. Nor is the book just for two-handed players. I have a strong suspicion that, after reading this book, many one-handers will not want to play one-handed anymore!

As an instructional book, *Two-Handed Tennis* is truly complete. It contains all the information you need to develop your own two-handed game, including tips on grips, footwork and strategy. The writing is accompanied by sequences of instructional photographs as well as photographs of two-handed pros in action. In short, nothing has been overlooked.

If you are as interested in improving your performance on the court as I am, you will surely enjoy this book. It is well organized, easy to read, and filled with so much knowledge and information that I seem to discover something new and important every time I pick it up. Let me know if you agree!

Kathy Rinaldi

PREFACE

I first experienced stroking a tennis ball two-handed in 1975, after injuring my arm while attempting to serve a little too hard. I had suffered a severely pulled deltoid muscle. In the days following this episode, while courageously attempting to teach my students, I discovered that it was even more painful to hit a backhand than a serve, due to the way in which the deltoid contracts on the backhand.

The preceding year I had begun teaching at a tennis school in San Francisco where my fellow instructors taught the two-handed backhand to many of our students, and I too began to acquire the intricacies of teaching the two-handed game. Equipped with this new knowledge, I decided to learn the two-hander myself because when I first experimented with it, I noticed that despite the damaged muscle, hitting a backhand didn't seem to hurt at all.

Since the time of this "blessing in disguise," my faith in the two-handed method has grown by leaps and bounds as I've personally witnessed how it furthered the progress of the hundreds of people I have had the privilege of instructing. In comparison with students who have insisted (against my advice) upon adopting the one-handed backhand, the two-handers have learned their particular stroke at a greatly accelerated rate and have, in my opinion, acquired a technique that ultimately will allow them to achieve a higher standard of play.

Through the years, some of my more avid students have asked me to recommend a book that might serve to augment their private lessons. I could only inform them that there wasn't a book designed to illuminate the special shot-making skills and strategies of the two-handed player. Although there have been many fine tennis books published over the course of the last fifty years, not one has addressed itself to the unique concerns of the ever-growing contingent of two-handers. As a matter of fact, the two-handed method has been largely ignored throughout the tennis literature, having been touched upon only very briefly and superficially in a few books.

It was at this time that I first seriously considered filling this void. The result, *Two-Handed Tennis: How to Play a Winner's Game*, is the product of eight years of two-handed teaching experience, including hundreds of hours of study and analysis of this ever more prevalent style of play. It is directed not only to two-handers but also to the many one-handers out there who would like to give the two-handed method a try.

I have attempted to present as many alternatives as possible (except for techniques that are clearly ineffective) in all facets of two-handed play, rather than to insist dogmatically upon a rigid adherence to just one approach. As evidenced by the considerable degree of diversity in the style of the top two-handers, contrasting techniques can certainly be employed to take a player to the top of the heap. I feel that as long as something works for a number of successful players it cannot be discounted. This effective and wide variety of technique is actually part and parcel of the two-handed method; you can do more with it to begin with. There are some strokes and styles, of course, that I personally prefer to others, and I do not hesitate to make these preferences known. But I feel that the student should be exposed to the pros and cons of all the possibilities residing in the two-handed universe; then the individual is in an ideal position to determine how techniques may best be combined and applied to construct an overall style of play. As everyone possesses differing abilities and goals, I feel it is important that students be free to choose from among worthy alternatives those that are most suitable to themselves. Accordingly, I believe that this work truly is a thorough and comprehensive presentation.

Insofar as this book is directed specifically to two-handers, many aspects of tennis instruction normally covered in tennis books are deliberately omitted. This was not done because the author considered them unimportant or irrelevant to the two-hander. Rather, certain areas were overlooked with the understanding that this information and knowledge exists in abundance and can and *should* be obtained by studying any of the many classic instructional books available. (My choice as perhaps the best of the more current crop is *Tennis for the Future* by Vic Braden.) I chose to limit the scope of this book because I felt quite certain that there was little else I could add to the body of knowledge established by many former great teachers and players. For instance, matters receiving no attention in this book are the two shots that can only be hit one-handed—the overhead smash (on the forehand side) and, of course, the serve. Also not considered are detailed conditioning regimens designed to build speed, strength, and stamina, practice drills that develop skill in shot making, the psychological aspects of competitive tennis, systematic teaching programs, and tennis etiquette. Singles strategy, both in general and from the unique perspective of the two-hander, is discussed in considerable detail, while the game of doubles and doubles strategy, from the two-handed perspective, is mentioned only briefly. However, if you want to learn how to hit any of the two-handed shots used by the world's best two-handers, and how to combine them effectively in match play, then this is the book for you. And it is designed to fulfill this purpose for both beginners as well as more advanced players.

There are many differing opinions regarding tennis technique these days, as the wide range of existing tennis articles and books indicates. Today, in this advanced age of scientific investigation, there is an ever-increasing trend toward objective verification of tennis theory in the wake of the work done by Vic Braden, Dr. Jack Groppel, and others. Many of the biomechanical properties attributed to various tennis strokes and techniques are theoretical. This doesn't mean, however, either that they're wrong or that they won't assist you in becoming a better tennis player, only that they have yet to be tested through experimentation. I hope that the ideas presented here will stimulate additional thought and subsequent analysis in academic and tennis research institutes, now that the means are available to do so. I know that the findings that result can only serve to further us all as participants or teachers of this great game. At any rate, it has been my experience that the two-handed method if studied and carefully applied, can enable a player to reach his or her highest possible level of competition, and it is for the development of all present and future two-handers that this work is intended.

ACKNOWLEDGMENTS

I'd like to acknowledge those who aided me, in a variety of ways, in completing *Two-Handed Tennis*. Steve Flink of *World Tennis* magazine, Kevin Diamond and Joan Penello of the Women's Tennis Association (WTA), and Amy Wishingrad of the Association of Tennis Professionals (ATP) all graciously expended time and energy to supply me with valuable statistics concerning the performance of many two-handed professional players.

My appreciation goes to Roger Ralphs of Los Angeles, and to Bill Horihan and Mick and Jan West, all of San Francisco, for reading and advising. Jan West must also be cited for some marathon and herculean typing performed on my behalf.

I'd like to thank Ursula Garvey of the Australian consulate in San Francisco for assisting me in acquiring photos of the original Australian two-handers from the *Sydney Morning Herald*, and to my friend Cheryl Traendly, for providing all of the wonderful photos of the contemporary two-handers as she was teaching me the importance of working with real professionals.

Dr. Jack Groppel of the University of Illinois generously shared his research concerning the two-handed method, and Dr. James Glynn provided his medical view of the physical benefits of playing two-handed.

My special thanks go to my literary agent, Fifi Oscard, of New York, for sharing my belief in the importance of *Two-Handed Tennis*, and to my personal editor and old friend, Craig Stephens of San Francisco. "Dreadnaught" unconditionally supported me in this endeavor but didn't push me when I was faltering. He never lost faith in me, even when I lost faith in myself, knowing that all things come to fruition when they're meant to.

And lastly, I wish to express my deepest admiration and appreciation to all the great two-handed champions who are the focus of this book, for having the good sense and courage to succeed with the unorthodox before it became so fashionable. This book is dedicated to Tracy, Bjorn, Jimmy, Eddie, Andrea, Chris, Frew, Gene, and Harold. Thanks for all the enjoyment you've given me as spectator, and all the instruction I've received as a student of the two-handed game.

Two-Handed Tennis

CHAPTER ONE

THE PAST, PRESENT, AND FUTURE OF THE TWO-HANDED GAME

It's unknown how many two-handed tennis players there have been, or what the ratio of two-handers to one-handers has been. However, it's interesting to speculate. It is probable that from the time the game assumed its present form in the nineteenth century until the mid-1970s, one-handers have outnumbered two-handers by perhaps 1000 to 1. The leading figure here may even be larger! Now this tremendous imbalance is beginning to decrease. The game is always changing, and the single most significant transition of the last decade has been the large increase in the number of two-handed players. There are currently more professional players utilizing the two-handed method than in the entire history of the sport. And on both public courts and in tennis clubs throughout the land, two-handers now abound!

THE GROWTH OF THE TWO-HANDED GAME

There are two primary reasons for the tremendous growth in the popularity of the two-handed style of play. The first is related to the explosive emergence of several two-handers who have risen to the very pinnacle of the professional game. First, American Jimmy Connors, and then Bjorn Borg of Sweden, with their two-handed backhand, came to dominate the men's game. Between 1972, when he turned pro, and 1978, the feisty and charismatic Connors won roughly half (48 percent) of the tournaments he entered, including Wimbledon and the U.S. Open in 1974, and the Open again in 1976 and 1978. He has won ninety-eight tournaments—more than any other male during the open era of tennis—and had amassed over $4 million in prize money through 1982.

Bjorn Borg won Wimbledon an unprecedented five straight times from 1976 to 1980, as well as six French Open titles from 1974 to 1981, and he held down the world's number one ranking from 1979

1

to 1981. The Swede hasn't done too poorly financially either, having won over $3.5 million in a relatively short career. And in terms of winning percentages, during this period both of these players are among the winningest in history, with Borg winning 75 percent of his pro matches, while Jimmy can boast of an unbelievable 89 percent. Is it any wonder that Connors was ranked number one on the Association of Tennis Professionals' (ATP) computer every single week but one from the summer of 1974 to the summer of 1979? By 1982, at the age of thirty, he had recaptured both Wimbledon and the U.S. Open titles, and had regained the world's number one ranking.

Similarly, American Chris Evert Lloyd has dominated the women's professional game for nearly the entirety of her career. She has been ranked number one in the world by the Women's Tennis Association in seven out of the last nine years. Between 1973 and 1981, Chris won a phenomenal 91 percent of her matches, while capturing 60 percent of the tournaments she entered. These figures are far superior to any other woman professional's during these years. In addition, she holds the all-time women's professional record for tournament victories with 120, and has also banked in excess of $4 million. Major career victories include Wimbledon in 1974, 1976, and 1981, the U.S. Open from 1975 to 1978, and 1980, and the French Open title in 1974, 1975, 1979, and 1980. In 1982, this very gracious and popular competitor again took the U.S. Open title. Chris is currently ranked number two in the world and is certainly a contender for the top spot in any year.

Two-handed American teenager Andrea Jaegar has risen to the number three position in the world rankings. She was the 1981 U.S. Clay Courts Champion and a Wimbledon semifinalist in 1982. Andrea holds the distinction of being the only player to defeat Chris Evert Lloyd three times in 1982. Everyone agrees that, as far as this friendly and outgoing seventeen-year-old is concerned, the sky is the limit. The 1980s may someday be recalled as the Jaegar decade in women's tennis; there's no doubt that she's going to secure her share of the major titles.

Another two-handed backhander, twenty-year-old Tracy Austin of Rolling Hills, California, is currently ranked number four in the world, although she was ranked number two in 1979, 1980, and 1981. Tracy won a remarkable 85 percent of her matches between 1979, when she turned pro at the age of fifteen, and 1981, and had earned more than $1.7 million through 1982. After setting the U.S. junior record for the most age group titles with twenty-five, she became the youngest player ever to win a professional tournament and, at the age of sixteen, the youngest ever to win the U.S. Open (1979).

Also in 1979, she took the Italian Open, and in the process snapped Chris Evert Lloyd's string of 125 straight clay court victories in the semifinals. In 1980, while only eighteen, she became the youngest millionaire athlete in the history of sport and occupied the top spot in the rankings during that summer. In 1981 she recaptured the U.S. Open, defeating Martina Navratilova in the finals. In addition, she is the only women to hold a lifetime edge over Chris Evert Lloyd (nine victories and seven defeats) and can also boast of a 6–1 career edge over Andrea Jaegar. Through the better part of 1982, the intelligent and thoughtful Ms. Austin was severely hampered by back and shoulder injuries, but when she's healthy again you can expect her to make a strong run at the top position, too.

Now, stop for just a moment and consider Connors's, Borg's, Evert Lloyd's, and Austin's statistics, and you will realize just how extraordinary is the success which they represent, especially in light of the fact that there are so many fine players in the field at every professional tournament.

The other major reason for the meteoric rise in popularity of the two-handed method is closely related to the first: It is obviously a tremendously effective way to stroke a tennis ball! One can have no doubt upon observing these champions that the two-hander is a highly formidable weapon. Not only do they drive the ball with tremendous force, but they also possess deadly accuracy. We've all witnessed, with awe, their amazing ground-stroking consistency; they win because they miss much less often than their opponents.

THE PAST—AUSTRALIAN ROOTS

What are the roots of the two-handed game? Who are the predecessors of these contemporary stars and when did these forerunners first appear on the international tennis scene? As every aficionado of the game knows well, tennis owes a great deal to the Australians. They have contributed so much in the way of great players, coaches, and tradition that it should not come as too great a surprise to discover that "down under" lies the cradle of the two-handed shot.

Vivian McGrath

The first player of world-class caliber ever to use a two-handed shot was an Australian, Vivian McGrath. As a matter of fact, it is generally agreed that his two-hander was one of the greatest shots of all time. Fellow Australian two-hander Geoff Brown said (in J. Pollard [ed.], *Lawn Tennis the Australian Way,* Melbourne: Lansdowne

Vivian McGrath in the finals of the 1940 Australian Open, slicing the backhand approach shot. *(John Fairfax & Sons, Ltd.)*

Press, 1963), "I would class McGrath's two-handed stroke on the left side ahead of the Donald Budge backhand, which is next." Although he is not among the all-time greats, Vivian held several important singles titles, including the Australian singles title of 1937, and he also played on five Australian Davis Cup Squads. He won Australian, Italian, German, and French doubles titles with partner and fellow countryman Jack Crawford. In actuality, he is best remembered not for this record in competition, but rather for his role in catalyzing a two-handed tennis boom in his native land. It was natural that many youngsters would choose to emulate McGrath, because at the onset of his career he was winning consistently with a powerful topspin backhand, which he hit, of all things, with both hands. In the thirties and forties, two-handers began popping up all over just like kangaroos. Unfortunately, he faded rather quickly from the international tennis scene, never attaining the tennis immortality that several of the game's pundits predicted. It has been said that McGrath became "over-tennised" and subsequently burned out while still in his early twenties. He later went on to become a successful and popular coach in Australia.

John Bromwich, pictured in the 1947 White City tournament in Sydney, returning serve from the open stance in the deuce court. (*John Fairfax & Sons, Ltd.*)

John Bromwich

John Bromwich was one of the many young Australians who copied McGrath's two-handed style. He soon went on to become one of the stellar performers of the late 1930s and the entire 1940s. As a matter of fact, he was ranked number two in the world in 1939, the year that he won the Australian Open. And like his idol McGrath, Bromwich made significant contributions to his country's Davis Cup efforts, competing a total of seven times. His similarity to McGrath does not end there, though, for his career was also curtailed, but in a slightly different way. John spent five years in the armed forces during World War II, and consequently was out of competition during his peak playing years of twenty-one to twenty-six. But for this hiatus, he undoubtedly would have claimed many more important international titles, including the major titles—Wimbledon, the U.S. Open, the French Open, and the Australian.

He was also a most unusual player in that he was a natural right-hander who trained himself to play left-handed. His left-handed, two-handed backhand did not possess the awesome power of most two-handed shots because he preferred to use an unusually short backswing. Nevertheless, with his great control, fleetness of foot, and tenacity Bromwich became a real standout. His patient baseline style was quite similar to that of Harold Solomon, a popular and well-known contemporary two-hander who has often been ranked among the world's top ten players. Like "Solly," Bromwich possessed a relatively weak serve and had to rely almost exclusively on his ground strokes. In other words, he won most of his matches by simply outsteadying his opponents; he was extremely patient and didn't miss very often. Unlike Solomon, though, he was a very temperamental individual whose play was frequently characterized by severe emotional outbursts directed at himself when his performance fell short of his lofty expectations. Tennis historians generally consider Bromwich to be one of the game's all-time great doubles players, too.

Geoff Brown

The next major Australian to join the two-handed tennis boom was Geoff Brown. Interestingly enough (and reminiscent of Bjorn Borg, whose backhand was an offshoot of his hockey slap shot), Brown's two-hander actually evolved out of a cricket shot, and consequently

Geoff Brown—winning the 1945
New South Wales Hardcourt
Open—playing the two-handed
backhand drop volley on a clay
court. (John Fairfax & Sons, Ltd.)

he sported an even more unorthodox style than Bromwich. Known as a power player, Brown was a big, strong right-hander who developed a two-handed forehand that he hit with his left hand on the bottom of the handle. As a result, he was forced to hit his one-handed backhand with the right hand a considerable distance up the racquet handle, thus greatly restricting his reach. Eventually finding this unacceptable, Brown finally chose to completely discard the backhand and develop a one-handed, left-handed forehand. He successfully mastered this difficult transition and won several international titles. His proudest achievement was to reach the finals of Wimbledon in 1946, losing in five tough sets to Yvon Petra of France. Brown was also an outstanding doubles player, arriving four times in the Wimbledon finals.

Pancho Segura

Next, from South America, rather than Australia, came one of the game's great stylists—the colorful Pancho Segura. Pancho's style of play somewhat resembled Geoff Brown's original approach; Segura also used a right-handed, two-handed forehand with his left hand placed below his right. However, instead of a left-handed forehand, he hit an orthodox one-handed backhand with the hand near the bottom of the handle. This forehand grip required Pancho to make a very difficult switch when alternating between his two ground strokes. After hitting a backhand, the right hand had to be moved to an upper position for the forehand or shifted to the lower position for a backhand, after stroking a forehand. As you can well imagine, these cumbersome grip changes are a bit like juggling, and many still wonder how Pancho was able to change so quickly.

As a youngster, Segura emigrated to the United States from Ecuador and attained initial prominence by winning the NCAA Tennis Championships in 1942, 1943, and 1944, playing for the University of Miami. Later, as a pro, he defeated Pancho Gonzales 6–2, 6–2, 6–2 at the 1952 U.S. Open. Perhaps his greatest triumph was in 1958 at the advanced tennis age of thirty-seven. On consecutive days, he beat Lew Hoad, Gonzales, Frank Sedgeman, Tony Trabert, Rex Hartwig and Ken Rosewall—the very cream of the crop of this era—to take the Masters crown in Los Angeles.

With his more recent participation on the grand masters circuit during the 1970s, Pancho's playing career spans the better part of four decades. He has also developed into one of the premier teachers in the game. His most famous protégé, Jimmy Connors, certainly credits Segura for some measure of his phenomenal success.

Here's Cliff Drysdale in his days as the player-coach of the San Diego Friars of World Team Tennis.

Cliff Drysdale

South African Cliff Drysdale is another in the line of distinguished two-handed players. In 1965, he burst into the limelight when he reached the finals of the U.S. Open, losing in four exciting sets to Manual Santana of Spain. In 1979, at the age of thirty-seven, Cliff was still ranked in the world's top fifty. Today, he is still competing on the Legends of Tennis Circuit along with the other top players of the fifties and sixties, when he is not doing an excellent job covering tennis matches on national television.

The Wave of the Future

Drysdale was the best two-hander to appear in the 1960s. In the 1970s many two-handers had emerged in both men's and women's tennis. Assessing this trend, it appears both natural and inevitable

Kathy Rinaldi playing the high backhand from the open stance on a clay court.

that there will be even more double-handed strokers in the 1980s. Indeed, if you analyze the Women's Tennis Association (WTA) statistics for 1982, you'll discover that eighteen (36 percent) of the world's top fifty women are two-handers. Ten years ago less than 5 percent were two-handers.

Sixteen-year-old Floridian Kathy Rinaldi became the youngest person ever to turn professional, in July 1981, at the ripe old age of fourteen. Earlier that same summer she had become the youngest individual to win a match at Wimbledon. By the end of 1982, she had climbed to the number thirteen position in the WTA rankings and established herself as the top new two-handed female player of the young decade. I think it would be a colossal understatement to say that Kathy has a great future ahead of her. You can look for this strong attractive young woman to crash the top ten in 1984.

Andrea Temesvari is a two-hander
who really feels comfortable at the
net. Here she is poised and ready
for the two-handed backhand
volley.

In addition to Ms. Rinaldi, there are several other young two-handed women who will certainly be heard from in the mid-1980s. Among the top contenders for stardom are: Bonnie Gadusek, nineteen, of the U.S., and ranked seventeen in the WTA in 1982; Andrea Leand, twenty, also an American, and ranked twenty in 1982; Catherine Tanvier, seventeen, of France, twenty-nine; Andrea Temesvari, sixteen, of Hungary, ranked thirty-one; Leigh Thompson, nineteen, of the U.S., ranked thirty-four; and Mary Lou Piatek, of the U.S., ranked forty-one in 1982. Of this young two-handed sorority, I feel that Temesvari is the most talented; she gets my vote as "most likely to succeed." She has already logged victories over Tracy Austin, Bettina Bunge, ranked nine, Virginia Ruzici, ten, and Kathy Rinaldi. The young Hungarian, in addition to her precocious poise and maturity, has all the shots, and at sixteen, all the time in

Sweden's Mats Wilander playing the wide one-handed backhand volley.

the world to fully perfect them. Another two-hander to look out for is Manuela Maleeva of Bulgaria who is ranked eleventh in 1986 but reached the number four spot in 1985. And then, of course, there is American Bennie Gadusek who cracked the world's top ten in 1986. When we begin to discuss stroke production, we'll have a good deal more to say about some of these exciting two-handed newcomers.

The brightest male star yet to appear on the decade's tennis horizon is eighteen-year-old Mats Wilander of Sweden. In 1982, while still just seventeen, he stood the tennis world on its ear when he defeated three of the world's best: Jose-Luis Clerc, Ivan Lendl, and Guillermo Vilas to capture his first major title at the French Open and establish himself as one of the premier clay court players in the world. Mats has the honor of being the youngest man ever to win a major championship. And by the end of 1982 he had staked out a spot in the world's top ten, at number seven, and given John

McEnroe, the world's top player a real scare before finally succumbing in five sets in one of the most exciting Davis Cup matches (the 1982 quarter-finals) in recent memory. As Mats has become more adept on faster court surfaces he has been able to up his ranking to an all-time high of number three in 1985, joining the sports true elite.

Mats has been followed into the top ten by several of his young compatriots, namely Anders Jarryd, ranked number six in 1985, Joakim Nystrom, ranked number eight in 1986, and two-time NCAA Champion, Mikael Pernfors out of the University of Georgia. Pernfors astonished everyone in 1986 by reaching the finals of the French Open and clearly signalling that he, too, is a young star on the rise. Sweden, with its two-handed tennis mafia, certainly rivals or perhaps now surpasses the United States as the world's greatest two-handed tennis nation. And we should not forget to mention America's hard hitting Aaron Krickstein, ranked number nine at the end of 1985.

It is apparent that the age of two-handed tennis is now upon us; it's big and getting bigger every year. And as Jimmy Connors himself has said (*Tennis Magazine,* April 1978), the two-handed game is "the wave of the future." In the next chapter we'll explore the primary reason for the incredible growth of the two-handed style—its natural superiority.

CHAPTER TWO
THE SUPREMACY OF TWO HANDS

I would like to begin this discussion of the pros and cons of the respective playing styles by emphasizing that it is not my intention to belittle the one-handed method. I have nothing but the greatest respect and admiration for the game's great champions, and I am fully aware of the fact that until the 1970s almost everyone had been a one-hander. That's history! I believe, however, that by adopting the more potent two-handed method, the majority of tennis players will reach a higher standard of play.

THE FOUR MAJOR ADVANTAGES OF TWO-HANDED TENNIS

There are four principal advantages derived from stroking a tennis ball with two hands. First, you have more power; second, and closely related to the first, there is the factor of greater control; third, there is the matter of heightened versatility; and finally, there is a greatly reduced susceptibility to injury.

Power and Greater Strength

There are several reasons for the additional strength of the two-handed shot. The most basic is the fact that the use of both shoulders, arms, wrists, and hands produces a shot that is more forceful than that produced by only one of each. What I shall term the push and pull alliance is responsible in part for the extraordinary power of almost every two-handed shot. Whereas the one-hander is merely pulling an arm through the shot, the two-hander is pulling with the leading or forward arm, and is also pushing with the following or rear arm. More muscle mass is activated in hitting the two-handed shot, so common sense dictates that it will be more powerful—and it is! Consequently, the two-handed method is also more forgiving. In other words, the two-hander is able to hit the ball late (too far behind), off balance without a sufficient weight transfer, on the run or off center, while losing relatively little power due to the extra force generated by using all of the upper torso.

Control

Greater Stability   Experiments conducted by Dr. Jack Groppel of the University of Illinois Biomechanics Laboratory have dramatically confirmed the widely held belief that the extra strength of the two-handed grip increases both the potential power and the accuracy of a shot. At first it might appear that the aspects of power and control are unrelated. This misunderstanding is fostered by statements alleging that a particular player is blessed with one but devoid of the other; that is, "he or she can hit it hard but can't control it." In actuality, these elements become closely intertwined through their common component—strength. If a player lacks the strength to apply adequate pressure to the grip at impact, shots are deprived of both force and accuracy. In theory, Groppel says, "adequate wrist strength to resist impact assures maximum conveyance of force from the forearm to the striking implement and then to the ball" (*A Kinematic Analysis of the Tennis One- and Two-Handed Backhand Driver in Highly Skilled Female Competitors,* doctoral dissertation, Florida State University, 1978). An inability to apply enough force to the grip at impact will cause the racquet head to torque (twist longitudinally in the hands), deflecting the ball weakly in an unwanted direction. Groppel's test results revealed that the wrists of one-handers oscillated to a much greater degree than those of the two-handers on the respective backhands, producing less solidity to counteract the tremendous force of impact. As the degree of oscillation increases, the acceleration of the wrist joint will decrease through the impact phase of the stroke, reducing hand and racquet acceleration proportionately.

This solidity is particularly valuable when attempting to return those extremely high-paced shots that can "jar" the racquet. The one-handed player is often simply unable to wield the racquet with enough authority to handle these bullets, especially when the racquet head torques on an off-center hit. On the other hand, the two-hander, with roughly twice the strength in the grip, stands a much better chance of withstanding the destructive force of a mis-hit and returning the ball into play. Interestingly enough, many one-handed players, even professionals, will occasionally slap their nondominant hand onto their racquet handle when near the net, in an attempt to return extremely hard hit volleys and overhead smashes. This action reflects an instinctive knowledge on their part that it is easier to blunt the destructive force of these devastating shots with the additional strength and stability of two hands.

The two-hander is also able to generate additional power through the active use of the wrists, without sacrificing control, due also to a

Kathy Rinaldi is blessed with excellent muscular development in the arms and upper body; she may be the strongest two-handed woman on the international scene. She will have no problem counteracting the force of impact on this wristy two-handed backhand.

stronger grip. On the other hand, the one-hander is less capable of hitting "wristy" shots accurately because it is much more difficult to control the racquet head with just one hand and wrist. Dr. Groppel found that one-handers, in order to compensate for a weaker grip, typically use about four times as much wrist flexion (forward displacement) as the two-hander to counteract the force of impact. But with less grip strength, they tend to lose control of the racquet head as the hitting arm straightens and the racquet head reaches higher velocities toward contact. This explains many one-handers' well-known tendencies to bend the arm and lead with the elbow on the backhand, or to bend the elbow excessively on the forehand and slap at the ball with only the wrist. In both cases this causes the ball to be contacted way too close to the body in an unconscious attempt to more securely absorb the shock of impact. Naturally, this can only lead to a critical decrement in torque and subsequent drastic reduction in the velocity of the shot. The extra gripping power of two hands, however, allows the ball to be contacted with the arms fully extended without any loss of racquet head control at upper acceleration values. Although it is demonstrated that the use of two hands means less wrist flexion needs to be used to bolster impact, when a good deal of wristiness is used for the sake of deception or for the production of topspin, the two-hander is better equipped to control the ball. (Chapter 8 will examine in detail the two-hander's marvelous capacity to utilize the wrists to great advantage.)

To further prevent the wrist from succumbing to the shock of impact, one-handers normally tend to contact the ball earlier (several inches more forward toward the net) than the two-hander, particularly on the backhand. The wrist has then traveled far enough to have accelerated sufficiently to more fully resist the trauma. The one-hander also contacts the backhand earlier because the stroke is hit with the anterior (forward) shoulder. On the other hand, two-handed shots always involve a movement employing the posterior (rear) shoulder and can thus be hit a little later (a little farther back from the net). This is an extremely important characteristic of two-handed stroke production, and a good deal more will be said later regarding the two-handers' capacity to take the ball later without seriously sacrificing either power or control.

Racquet Control

The capacity to control the racquet is also critical for accuracy. The two-hander possesses a greater degree of control over the racquet head, and therefore over the ball, due simply to the additional hand, arm, and shoulder complex, which increases the precision with which the racquet may be guided to the ball. As Vic Braden says, "Most players can't control the ball with one hand, so if you can learn control with two hands, I say great" (*Tennis for the Future*, Boston: Little, Brown, 1977). The Feldenkrais method, a discipline oriented toward health through expanded self-awareness, may be used to illuminate the dynamics of this fascinating phenomenon.

Moshe Feldenkrais, a Russian-born Israeli physicist and engineer, has developed a broad system of movement exercises designed to improve the functioning of the central nervous system and brain by increasing mental–physical self-awareness. Briefly described, the system is intended to increase the number of neuromuscular connections in order to expand the body's capacity for freer and more efficient motor function. When muscles operate they send messages through the afferent central nervous system pathways to the brain, which in turn relays messages back to the muscles via the efferent (motor) network in a continually upwardly spiraling cycle of heightened psychosomatic awareness and hence control. Control increases as new pathways are established and neuromuscular connections increase. In utilizing both sides of the upper body, the two-hander naturally creates many new connections allowing him or her to guide the strings to the ball with maximal accuracy. The Feldenkrais method is becoming increasingly popular among dancers, musicians, athletes, and others who rely on refined movement for their livelihood. If you're interested in delving further into this intriguing discipline, I suggest that you read *Awareness Through Movement,* which is full of Feldenkrais's simple but very powerful transformative exercises.

Easier to Groove   This heightened precision is intimately associated with the fact that the two-handed stroke is easier to groove and to keep grooved than a one-handed stroke. Any stroke, if it is to be maximally effective on an ongoing basis, must be produced consistently with virtually the same bodily movements time after time. If so—in tennis talk—it is said to be *grooved.* The racquet will then be taken back along the same path and be brought forward through the hitting area into the follow-through position along the same line each and every time, in much the same manner that any well-made mechanical device operates on each revolution, cycle, and so on.

Watch the good players in action and you will notice that any single stroke will be essentially identical every time. Of course, there will always be slight differences in, for example, a series of backhands, depending on whether the ball is hit down the line or cross-court, how close the ball is to the player's body, and the height at which it is played. Within rather strictly defined parameters, however, the skilled player is able to reproduce automatically that unique stroke which has become grooved through training. Grooving all the strokes is indispensable to success in tennis, for if a stroke is grooved and is also technically correct, consistency in shot-making is practically assured.

Occasionally, though, a player will lose confidence in a given stroke and bemoan his or her sudden inability to control the resulting shots. In other words, it has simply slipped out of its groove, so that the path of the stroke is varying excessively time after time; it has become erratic, and predictably, the shots have also become errant. This occurs rarely, however, if ever with a two-handed shot, due to the presence of an extra hand, arm, and shoulder that naturally increases the neuromuscular precision of the stroke.

Conversely, without the extra controlling presence of the nondominant arm, there is much greater potential for unwanted motion both horizontally and vertically. *In my teaching experience I have found that a one-handed stroke must normally be performed many more times than a two-hander before finally settling into a consistent pattern, prolonging the length of time required to fully learn it.*

When you talk about strokes that are really grooved, two names come most readily to mind: Jimmy Connors and Tracy Austin. Some observers would contend that they are indeed too mechanical or machinelike—especially Tracy. Nevertheless, to the eyes of the tennis coach who values this degree of sheer consistency, they are nothing short of poetry in motion. The players' original coaches, Gloria Connors of Belleville, Illinois, and Robert Lansdorp of Los Angeles, respectively, deserve tremendous credit for painstakingly developing some of the most beautifully grooved and mechanically efficient strokes that have ever been encountered on a tennis court.

Not only are their two-handed backhands precisely grooved, but so are their one-handed forehands. Is it perhaps conceivable that the tremendous natural regularity of their two-handers provided them with the sense (on the sensory-motor level) of what it *must* be like to have an almost equally grooved one-hander? This is certainly an issue that begs to be addressed by the new wave of tennis researchers. If it turns out to be true, it is certainly a serendipitous benefit of any two-handed stroke. In other words, despite the acquisitional imbalance between one- and two-handed strokes, the two-hander may actually reinforce and accelerate the one-handed learning process to a considerable degree.

Controlled Power   It is becoming apparent that the use of two hands, arms, and shoulders is superior when it comes to stroking a fast-moving tennis ball within the confines of a relatively small area—a tennis court. The two-handed method yields the greatest power combined with the highest potential for harnessing it. Remember though, a successful tennis player always learns first to control the ball, keeping it in play consistently, and then gradually increases the amount of pace that his or her accurate shots contain.

Feel and Touch   *Feel* and *touch* are terms often heard in conversations between experienced tennis players. They are somewhat vague and perhaps a little difficult to define, but let's give it a try anyway. They refer to the sensation one has when one solidly feels the ball on the strings and can then accurately direct it to a particular point in the court. The sensation is, of course, experienced in the brain, but physically it initiates in the hands and is centered there. Just as two arms yield greater awareness and accuracy in the movement of the racquet, two hands are also able to capture more sensation and communicate more of it to the brain. Ask any two-hander and he'll testify that there is more feel and therefore more control with a two-handed shot than with a one-hander.

Interestingly, in other activities in which control is paramount, two hands are also utilized. For example, have you ever noticed the manner in which the police in our contemporary television and motion picture crime dramatizations fire their handguns? More often than not, we see both hands wrapped around the butt. And there is also an example from basketball. Rick Barry, now retired but formerly with the Houston Rockets and the Golden State Warriors, was one of the outstanding professional basketball players of the 1970s. On the court big Rick could truly do it all, and perhaps the most intriguing thing about his play was the way he shot free throws. During his professional career, he was the only player to use both hands at the foul line. His 89.6 percent average is the highest in the history of the National Basketball Association!

Versatility

Greater versatility constitutes the third major advantage of the two-handed style. The two-hander is capable of hitting a wider range of shots effectively, primarily due to the ease with which varying degrees of topspin can be produced (*topspin* is the rotary motion given to a ball that makes it rotate forward in the direction in which it is traveling). *Topspin is so much easier to apply with the additional strength of two hands that facilitates a greater vertical lift of the racquet up and through the ball.* In this regard, it is interesting to note that many coaches I've encountered who teach the one-handed method exclusively, occasionally deploy the two-hander to give the student the feeling for what it must be like to dramatically lift up to the ball. They have, of course, discovered that with the strength of only one side of the upper body, many student-players have difficulty attaining the degree of vertical lift, and hence topspin, that all two-handers merely take for granted. I have to assume that the only thing that inhibits them from actually creating two-handed strokes intentionally is either force of habit or a rigid adherence to outmoded tennis teaching dogma.

Greater strength for offensive topspin potential is, of course, the prime reason that so many women, in general, and women professionals, in particular, utilize the two-handed backhand. At this point, however, I want to make it abundantly clear that I am not saying that the two-handed method is suited only to women. On the contrary, a couple of gentlemen named Connors and Borg would certainly take exception to that contention; even such muscular specimens gain additional topspin power potential with two hands.

Along with this capacity to produce a lot of topspin, the two-hander is also best equipped—through strength of grip and related control of the racquet head—to deceptively alter the direction of a topspin shot with a last-second flexion of the wrists. This is, of course, much more difficult to do successfully with just one hand. Consequently, only the strongest and most gifted one-handers, those competing on or near the highest levels of play, are able to hit the variety of topspin shots as effectively as the typical two-hander. In chapter 4 the two-hander's complete arsenal of shots will be presented and analyzed in full detail.

Reduced Susceptibility to Injury

The last significant advantage of the two-handed style concerns the matter of health. For some players, this may be the most important reason of all for adopting the two-handed style. Many orthopedists firmly believe that the use of both hands may be instrumental in either preventing or eliminating certain arm injuries prevalent among tennis enthusiasts. The most common of these is, of course, the infamous tennis elbow, the scourge of players of every era in all parts of the globe. The following is a statement by Dr. James J. Glynn, a former Assistant Professor of Orthopedic Surgery at the University of California, San Francisco, who was also team physician for the Denver Broncos professional football team. He now practices in Petaluma, California.

I. Introduction

Does hitting a two-handed backhand reduce the incidence of lateral epicondyle extensor tendonitis, better known as tennis elbow? The following are my personal observations, research and discussion with other orthopedic surgeons here in the San Francisco Bay area.

II. Prevention

Irritation of the extensor muscle tissue over the lateral portion of the elbow is a very common problem in tennis players. It is not confined to this group, however, and in fact is often found in other individuals whose activities require repetitive use of an arm; usually those requiring repeated striking of an instrument such as a hammer. Thus, carpenters often suffer from tennis elbow.

Various theories have been advanced regarding the cause(s). The main common theme seems to revolve around repetitive use and strain of the extensor musculature of the forearm resulting eventually in a chronic inflammation of the muscle group located above the elbow. This strain and subsequent inflammation is much more likely to result from hitting a one-handed backhand than a forehand, due to the more dynamic manner in which the muscles contract on the former. It can vary in severity from minor irritation after a long match or workout, to incapacitating pain in which even lifting a pad of paper is associated with noticeable discomfort.

III. Prevention

This leads to the possibility that if one is able to reduce the frequency or force of these repetitive contractions, one could reduce the chances of incurring tennis elbow. Certainly the length of a tennis match cannot be reduced. So we must consider the ways in which, with each backhand, the force generated by the extensor mechanism can be reduced. The most obvious solution is to hit the stroke with two hands. Many other activities that require the stroking or hitting of a ball with an intermediary object, such as baseball or golf, have a negligible incidence of tennis elbow symptoms. This is primarily due to the fact that when both arms are used, the resulting shock of the impact is dispersed over twice as much musculature and bone tissue, naturally leading to a significant decrease in the trauma experienced by a single muscle or muscle groups.

IV. Conclusion

In the past seven years, I have questioned all of my patients with tennis elbow as to how they hit a backhand. I have not encountered a single two-handed backhand player with tennis elbow. Likewise, none of the other orthopedists whom I have consulted have unearthed a case of tennis elbow in a player with a two-handed backhand. There seems to be no question that the two-handed backhand prevents this problem and should be adopted by one-handers experiencing pain and subsequent reduction in shot-making proficiency.

The Dual Two-Handed Approach

Although I am not a physician, I think that it makes good sense to encourage those individuals with any sort of chronic wrist, elbow, or shoulder problems to adopt the dual two-handed style (two hands for every shot). If the discomfort greatly limits your enjoyment and/or effectiveness, or if it has forced you to give up the game entirely, why not learn to hit all your shots with both hands? If this is your situation, what have you got to lose? With both halves of the upper torso to absorb the shock of impact, there is an excellent chance that you may not experience your former level of discomfort. In fact, the pain may never reappear.

A CANDID CRITIQUE OF THE TWO-HANDED STYLE

Now that we have detailed the many advantages to be derived from employing the two-handed style, I think it only fair to play the devil's advocate and consider its lone liability. The major criticism always leveled at the two-handed game is that it prevents one from reaching quite as far as with one hand. The maximum radius of the latter stroke is about 6 to 8 inches greater, the exact amount depending on your size. (The larger you are, and the longer your arms are, the greater this figure becomes, and the farther you can reach in an absolute sense.) This means that there will always be a small percentage of balls that can only be played by letting go with the nondominant arm and stroking one-handed. This slight reduction in reach requires the two-hander to compensate with greater quickness and anticipation as well as with superior conditioning so as to hit as few one-handers as possible. The quicker you become, and the more accurately you can determine where the opponent's shots are going to go, the fewer you'll have to hit. As a junior player, Chris Evert Lloyd confronted this issue in a positive way; in an article in *Tennis Annual* (1977) she wrote, "The thing I'm always conscious of when I'm practicing is moving my feet quickly. That way, I can set up for the shot and be balanced and not have to lunge for it."

The top professional two-handers are among the fastest on the entire circuit; Connors, Borg, Solomon, Dibbs, Evert Lloyd, Mayer, Austin, and Jaegar are well above the mean in their ability to cover the court. Some have suggested that they were born with quick feet and have been able to succeed with two hands only because of this gift. Personally, I believe that they were forced to become a little quicker in order to use two hands, and that this very same motivational factor will work similarly for all other two-handers as well. In other words, if you know that in order to hit your best shot, the two-hander, you'll have to reach that wide ball a little sooner, then through sheer determination you will. *Will* is the key word here, for it is basically a matter of desire.

Although the very best double-handers are forced to hit very few one-handers with the quickness they've developed, there will always be a few shots that even the fleetest can't retrieve two-handed. Therefore, it is very important to become as adept as possible in hitting the occasional one-handed backhand (or forehand if you play with a two-handed forehand). In the final chapter, we'll have a lot more to say about the necessity of acquiring this versatility.

All in all, I firmly believe that the multiple advantages of the two-handed method far outweigh this solitary drawback. This is particu-

Like most of the two-handed base-
liners, Andrea Jaegar not only has
great quickness but also tremendous stamina and endurance that,
coupled with determination, enable
her to run the ball down all day
long.

larly true in light of the fact that when forced to play a shot while
lunging to full extension, two-handers are actually at no greater disadvantage than one-handers, because it is difficult for anyone to hit
an aggressive shot from such a defensive position. I think Vivian Mc-
Grath sums it up quite well (in J. Pollard [ed.], *Lawn Tennis the
Australian Way,* Melbourne: Lansdowne Press, 1963): "For most
people, anticipation can make up for any lack of reach it causes, and
it packs some tremendous advantages in arduous match play because
of the improved control it gives on ground strokes." Even as staunch
an advocate of traditional one-handed tennis instruction as Vic Braden says (in *Teaching Children Tennis the Vic Braden Way,* Boston:
Little, Brown, 1981), in discussing the value of two-handed strokes
to children, "The reduced reach on the two-handed shot is compen-
sated for by the fact that your child has virtually two forehands."
What! He says the two-handed is really a forehand? In chapter 3
we'll find out exactly what jocular Vic means.

Psychological Dependency

Other detractors have claimed that the two-handed method also creates a state of psychological dependency difficult to break when one "progresses" and can subsequently discard the shot in favor of a one-hander. I recall the many times during the latter half of 1974 that members of the press asked Bjorn Borg, the rising teenage superstar and winner of that year's French Open, when he would start using a one-handed backhand. He replied confidently that he would never switch over because he knew for certain that the two-hander was the best.

CHAPTER THREE
THE TWO-HANDED BACKHAND VERSUS THE TWO-HANDED FOREHAND

The preceding chapter compared the effectiveness of two hands with one hand and found that the two-handed method grants the greatest power and versatility, combined with the highest potential for controlling them. This chapter will contrast the two-handed backhand with the two-handed forehand and discover why there are so few of the latter and so many of the former.

THE BACKHAND BLUES

Most teaching pros would agree that the typical one-handed player's greatest difficulty is in developing an aggressive one-handed topspin backhand. If polled, I think that most one-handers would have to admit that their forehand is their stronger shot and that, by comparison, their backhand is considerably weaker. Below the top professional level, there are relatively few players who have a more effective one-handed backhand than forehand. Even among the pros who play one-handed, how many have better backhands than forehands? Only a handful.

Clearly, if you are one of the tennis multitudes singing the infamous "backhand blues," the addition of a more aggressive two-handed backhand will allow you to develop a better balanced and more potent game. Let's face it, your opponent knows as well as you that intelligent tennis is always based on attacking the other guy's weaknesses. If you combine an aggressive two-handed backhand with an existing strong one-handed forehand, where can that assault be directed? With the addition of this new weapon to your game, you may be able to walk out onto a court a month or two from today and rout that old archrival who has dealt you so many beatings in the past. Actually, I've heard this exact story from many of my students, formerly of the one-handed persuasion.

As a matter of fact, this is exactly what Association of Tennis Pro-

Paul McNamee is returning an extremely hard-hit smash. Even though he's a little off balance and is also hitting the ball a little "late," with the strength and solidity of two hands he'll at least get the ball back over the net.

fessionals (ATP) pro Paul McNamee did a few years back. In 1979 Paul was floundering with a ranking in the nineties on the ATP computer. He was right on the verge of retiring from tennis and entering law school in his native Australia. However, Paul didn't quit because he knew in his heart that if he was somehow able to shore up that old backhand weakness of his he could certainly do a lot better on the international circuit. So he took about six months off and learned a two-handed backhand under the tutelage of former Australian Davis Cup coach, the venerable Harry Hopman. Paul worked hard, often putting in as many as eight hours a day under the hot Florida sun. A year later, when he stunned John McEnroe at the French Open, it was apparent that his dedication and hard work were really going to pay off. And then, just a few months later, he teamed with countryman Peter McNamera to take the Wimbledon doubles crown. In 1982 they recaptured it. As Paul's singles performance has also continued to improve, he found himself ranked twenty-seven in the world in the latter part of 1981. This represents a jump of over sixty points in the rankings!

Chris Evert Lloyd has turned her shoulders so much on this two-hander that her opponent will see her back.

THE MORE POWERFUL FOREHAND

There are several biomechanical reasons why the forehand stroke is naturally more powerful than the backhand. First, the powerful pectoral or chest muscle on the body's dominant side (the right-hander's right side, the left-hander's left side) functions to generate more force on the forehand than the backhand. Second, the hitting shoulder's posterior position allows it to rotate farther and more dynamically than on the backhand. There is also a greater natural hip rotation on the forehand as they turn in unison with the shoulders. Furthermore, with the hitting shoulder in a position on the side of the body where the ball will be struck, one need only turn about 90 degrees to place this shoulder in the correct hitting position for a forehand. However, this shoulder is on the opposite side from where the backhand will be played and so must rotate considerably farther,

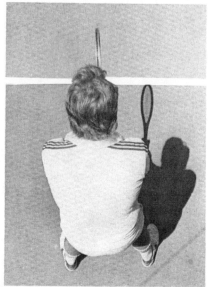

1. To hit the forehand, the dominant (right) shoulder need turn only about 90 degrees.
2. A view of the position of the shoulders from above, in the ready position.
3. To hit the backhand, the dominant (right) shoulder must turn about 120 degrees to maximize the power of the shot.

approximately 120 degrees to assume the optimal stroking position. Unfortunately, many one-handers, fearing that they can't time the ball with a full backswing, never learn to make a full 120 degree turn. Consequently, their backhands are rendered impotent by the restricted backswing because the racquet head cannot build sufficient momentum in moving this relatively short distance. The stroke is also deprived of the torque accruing from the rotation of the trunk; it contains only the limited power generated by the hitting limb.

Many one-handers have remedied their weak backhand conditions by switching to the two-hander. It not only produces a full shoulder turn—naturally—as the rear shoulder forces its forward counterpart to turn fully and in unison with it, but it also incorporates the many features that make the forehand such a potent movement. After all, the two-handed backhand can also be conceived of as a nondominant side forehand with an additional hand, arm, and shoulder thrown in (for extra strength, support, and balance). The pectoral muscle on the nondominant side can then function in the same dynamic manner that it does on a forehand. The nondominant side posterior shoulder, with its greater degree of rotation, will increase the force of the shot as does the greater natural hip rotation accompanying strokes employing the posterior arm and shoulder.

The baseball and golf swings are not so dissimilar from the tennis forehand that they cannot be used to illustrate this point. In actuality, they both rely heavily on an essentially forehandlike movement. Consequently, right-handed batters and golfers both stand to the left of the ball (leading with the nondominant arm) to full capitalize on the greater power potential of the posterior arm and shoulder to drive out and through (baseball) or down and through the ball (golf) to provide the bulk of the power. If, on the other hand, the backhand motion was more powerful, wouldn't these athletes strike the ball from the right side?

The forehandedness of the two-handed backhand escalates its potency in yet another important way. Through the operation of the posterior shoulder, the ball can and should be contacted later than a one-hander—at a point even with or just a few inches in front of the forward foot. This gives the two-hander more time to prepare for the shot. In other words, the racquet's forward acceleration to the ball can be started a fraction of a second later. On any level of play, but particularly on the higher levels, a two-hander is much less likely to suffer a severe loss of power from hitting late—even when dealing with those extremely hard to hit shots.

Conversely, the one-hander has less time to prepare for the ball because the hitting shoulder-arm is closer to the net and must, there-

1. The contact point for the one-handed backhand is at a point 12 to 18 inches ahead of the forward foot. Notice also that most of the hand is positioned in front of the handle and therefore provides less support than the forehand grip.

2. The contact point for any two-handed shot is even with or just slightly ahead of the forward foot.

fore, begin the stroke sooner to contact the ball the required 12–18 inches in front. Consequently, the one-handed player is much more likely to lose power by contacting the ball late—especially, again, on those big boomers.

A stroke employing the rear shoulder also guarantees a greater natural weight transfer and therefore heightened power potential. Why? The more efficient operation of the trunk causes more sheer body mass to flow forward at impact. Dr. Groppel believes this to be one of the most important factors for the production of two-handed power. His experiments indicate that the torso operates distinctly differently in strokes employing the front, as opposed to the rear shoulder. For the two-handed backhand, he found that the axis of rotation occurred around the spinal column to generate a more dynamic trunk rotation during the impact phase of the stroke. This also results in a more uniform body rotation with both arms and the trunk functioning as a single unified segment—in synchronization. *Thus, an accomplished two-hander has the feeling that he or she is stroking the ball with one corporate arm, not two.*

Conversely, Dr. Groppel also discovered that on the one-handed backhand, the arm rotates around the position of the hitting shoulder, causing the arm to operate independently of the torso to produce less torque in the trunk accompanied by a lower overall coordination of elements. He also concludes that this greater uniformity of upper-body movement is primarily responsible for the greater ease of learning the two-hander.

THE MORE FAMILIAR FOREHAND

The forehand is not only a more powerful stroke, it is also much easier for most people to learn because it is so similar to many other previously acquired movements. Stop and think, for just a moment or two, of all the activities we perform daily which are similar to the forehand stroke. Nearly all take place on the dominant side of the body, using the dominant arm. An excellent example of this is the nearly invariable tendency to pull a door closed with a forehand-type movement. Likewise, when opening a window or lifting an object from the ground, or simply eating food from a plate you are performing actions akin to the forehand. The list of such common "forehandlike" activities performed by and on one's dominant side is virtually endless and I'm sure that you can think of a few also. Can you imagine how strange it would be to see someone using a backhandlike movement to do any of the above mentioned things?

So, it is natural that individuals become more proficient at manipulating objects by and on their "educated," dominant sides. Consequently, when beginning to play tennis, most will adapt to the dominant side stroke more surely and confidently than to the backhand. Here is yet another important reason for the fact that so many players develop ferocious forehands but possess only frail backhands. Undoubtedly, many players could benefit from the heightened motor control provided by another hand, arm, and shoulder.

THE STABLE FOREHAND

There is one additional reason for the greater strength of most forehands. It concerns the relative positions of the dominant, or bottom hand, on the forehand, as opposed to the backhand. On the forehand, it is positioned almost entirely behind the handle, whereas it is almost completely in front of the handle on the backhand. It thereby provides much more support and stability at impact on the

With the forehand grip, most of the hand and wrist are positioned behind the handle to provide much more support than on a backhand grip.

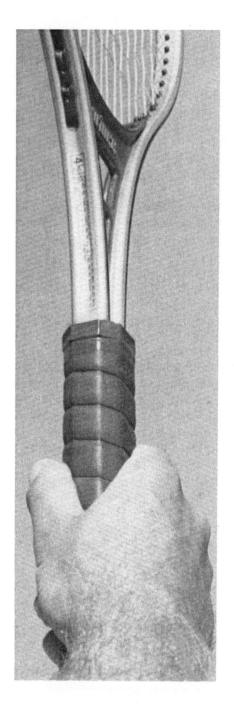

forehand. This partially explains Groppel's findings regarding the lower oscillation rates of the two-handed backhand. Certainly, the presence of the top, or nondominant, hand goes a long way to stabilizing the racquet at impact. Nevertheless, there is no doubt that a two-handed grip is stronger in general, and can for instance also buttress a weaker one-handed forehand grip.

SO WHY A TWO-HANDED FOREHAND?

Despite the overall superiority of the two-handed style, history contains the names of only a few top two-handed forehand players. It is quite apparent that the shot may never become as prevalent as the two-handed backhand, simply because most adults soon become satisfied with a one-handed forehand due to its natural ease, familiarity, and stability. In most cases it quickly becomes superior to the one-handed backhand which is then perceived as a weakness. So, it is the backhand that most players will first seek to improve by making the switch to two hands.

Nevertheless, the two-handed forehand cannot be ignored in light of the presence of names like Pancho Segura, Frew McMillan, and Gene Mayer. Certainly, it is the best choice of shots for certain individuals. If you are among the group of players unable either to control your forehand to your satisfaction or hit it offensively enough, I would enthusiastically recommend that you adopt the two-hander. It is sure to improve your game as it has others'.

Perhaps it is a bit unfortunate that most people become so quickly satisfied with their one-handed forehands. Recall the major advantages of the two-handed method. There is absolutely no reason why an average forehand could not be transformed into a good one, or why a good forehand could not become a great one by pursuing the two-hander. Who knows, by adopting the dual two-handed style, you might become the next great two-handed forehand player. Let's take a look at this special fraternity.

The Best Shot?

Until Gene Mayer rose to stardom, Pancho Segura was the best-known exponent of the two-handed forehand. No less a tennis authority than the all-time great Jack Kramer has nominated Segura's forehand as the best single shot ever seen on a tennis court. In order to beat Pancho, it was essential to keep the ball away from his forehand side. With this big weapon, he could completely control a match, hitting winners with uncanny regularity from any point on the court.

There are currently more professional players using the dual two-handed style than in the entire history of the game. American Gene Mayer moved into the number four position in the world singles rankings in 1981. He is now ranked fifth and was also chosen to represent his country in Davis Cup play in 1982. And then there is Frew McMillan of South Africa. One of the top doubles players of the past two decades, Frew has amassed an amazing ten major doubles titles since 1966, including five Wimbledon titles and three U.S. Open championships, as well as two French Opens. We'll have a good deal more to say about Frew when we discuss two-handed volleying techniques. And last, there is Hans Gildemeister of Chile, perennially ranked in the top fifty players in the world and reaching a career high of twenty-eight in 1982.

There is no doubt that the future will reveal many more practitioners of the totally dual-handed mode, or what might be termed "ho-

A recent picture of Pancho Segura hitting "the best shot."

listic tennis.'' And as those who win with it gain increasingly greater notoriety, many others will begin to emulate them. There will always be a tendency to follow the leaders. And as the use of the two-handed backhand continues to escalate, there will undoubtedly be a corresponding increase in the emergence of its counterpart. You'll hear people saying, ''If it works so well on the backhand, maybe it'll do just as much for my forehand.''

EARLY INITIATION INTO TENNIS

Another important advantage of the dual two-handed style is that it permits children to begin playing tennis at the earliest possible age and then to advance most rapidly. If you are at all familiar with the careers of many of the top two-handers such as Jimmy Connors,

Will Kevin Gottfried, son of famous one-hander Brian Gottfried, break with tradition and become a two-hander?

Chris Evert Lloyd, and Tracy Austin, you certainly understand the importance of an early initiation into the game. All of these current champs began banging the ball around before the age of six. (It is interesting to note that both Connors and Evert Lloyd had parents who were teaching pros.) It seems that most young tennis aspirants develop two-handed shots simply because they are unable to wield the racquet with only one hand. Regarding his compatriot, John Bromwich, Geoff Brown says (in J. Pollard [ed.], *Lawn Tennis the Australian Way*, Melbourne: Lansdowne Press, 1963): "The Bromwich two-hander stemmed from an inability at the age of seven to swing a heavy racquet properly with one hand." Vivian McGrath concurs (see Pollard, above): "I started that way because the racquet felt too heavy for me on that side; perhaps it was because I automatically felt I could get more control over the racquet by using two hands."

Actually, many youngsters even up to the age of ten or eleven initially encounter difficulty in stroking, primarily because they still lack the muscular development necessary to accurately guide the racquet to the ball. Consequently, they continuously mis-hit the ball, and their weak wrists are the cause of a radically dropped racquet head which invariably leads to loss of control. In addition, their weakness prevents them from bringing the racquet head through the hitting area with enough velocity to counteract the force of impact and drive the ball over the net. If their shots do occasionally clear the net, they do so just barely, fluttering through the air like wounded birds.

The stronger two-handed method largely counteracts these problems associated with youthful weakness. I find that when children are taught two-handed strokes, they contact a greater number of balls on the strings and hit more shots over the net, with greater pace, much sooner than kids attempting to learn one-handed strokes.

Even some smaller adults have relatively weak arms and wrists. The dual two-handed approach will also provide them with the strength and support essential for learning correct stroke production right from the outset.

SIMPLICITY OF SYMMETRY

An individual choosing the holistic approach receives the extra benefit of being able to groove the strokes more rapidly and surely than a two-handed stroke can be grooved in conjunction with a one-handed stroke, because the respective dual-handed strokes are identical. The learning that occurs on one side will serve to reinforce the learning that takes place with the other stroke. Accordingly, those employing the one-handed backhand and forehand normally experience the most difficulty because the strokes are the most dissimilar.

That's enough theory for now. Let's talk about some real tennis strokes; specifically, a pair of the best two-handed backhands from continent to continent.

CHAPTER FOUR

THE TWO MAJOR STYLES OF THE TWO-HANDED GROUND STROKES

No two tennis strokes are exactly the same; all the top two-handers hit their shot(s) somewhat differently. Nevertheless, there are two-handed strokes which are quite similar, in specific ways, to certain others. All of the world's top two-handers can be placed within one of two broad categorizations of style. Let us call one the flat or Jimmy Connors style and the other the topspin or Bjorn Borg style. In actuality, they are not as entirely divisible and separate as they may first appear to be. Every so-called flat shot will have some degree of forward rotation because it is nearly impossible to send a ball off the strings without any spin. There is, therefore, really no such thing as as perfectly flat shot, only shots that are flatter than others. It is illuminating to conceptualize the phenomenon of spin as occurring on a continuum ranging from shots with excessive spin, at one end, to shots with virtually no spin on the other. For the purposes of our discussion, the latter will be referred to as *flat*.

Connors and Borg have been chosen to represent the major styles of the two-handed shots, not solely for their extraordinary success, but also because each so closely epitomizes the classic form of his respective style. Connors's flat backhand is characterized by its extremely straight-line trajectory, great pace, and low bounce. Conversely, Borg's topspin backhand is a slower moving, higher bouncing shot with a much more arced trajectory. It is hoped that by understanding the advantages and disadvantages of each style, students of the two-handed game will gain the insight to determine which one they wish to develop.

THE FLAT STYLE

Any experienced tennis player can tell you that the flat drive is extremely difficult to return as forcefully as it is received. With its great pace and low trajectory, it passes from one side of the court in less

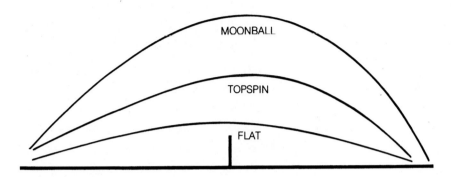

Trajectories—flat, topspin, and the moonball

time than any other type of shot. Consequently, there is less time in which to reach the ball and position yourself properly. You are often forced to commit an error or to answer with a very weak reply which the flat hitter can then "put away." If you've seen Jimmy Connors on the court, you undoubtedly know how devastating this daring style can be. He is capable, on any given stroke, of ending the point with a rocketing drive. The flat game is certainly the ultimate in offensive, aggressive, "take it to the limit" tennis.

Small Margin of Error
The flat style has one major drawback, however. The low trajectory of the shot is such that the ball must clear the net by a relatively small margin if it is to land safely within the court. In other words, the flat shot skims the top of the net. Naturally, many a flat ball ends up there. Or, if it is hit a little higher to avoid the net, it will often go long or wide out of court, if it contains even moderate pace. As has often been said, without topspin there is nothing to bring the ball down but gravity. It is inevitable then, that the player consistently employing the flat style will usually commit a higher number of unforced errors than a player utilizing more topspin.

THE TOPSPIN STYLE

Topspinners owe their remarkable consistency to the aerodynamic effects of topspin. As the ball is revolving forward and approaching the other side of the court, a condition of greater air pressure above the ball is created, causing it to drop. The more spin that is applied, the more quickly the ball will descend. The great value of top-

Bjorn Borg sending off another arcing, looping, high-bouncing backhand.

spin lies in the fact that the ball can be hit higher above the net and still descend safely into the court. Such a shot is said to have a high margin of safety over the net. Thus, with the great safety of the top-spin shot, it is not uncommon, when two topspin stylists such as Borg and Solomon square off, for the ball to travel over the net in excess of fifty times during a single point.

This sudden aerodynamic plunge also permits the ball to be angled more acutely. It can thereby be directed into a greater portion of the area in the court, where it is either more difficult or impossible to re-trieve. Let's take a look at the versatile two-hander's dazzling array of topspin shots.

Topspin Baseline Drives

As shown in the diagram, shots hit along a line extending from point A to points B or C will serve to extend the rally and keep the opponent tied to the baseline, B, or pull him or her out of position, opening the court for your next shot, C. These two shots, especially B, are normally central to players such as Borg, Evert Lloyd, or Austin's match strategy. They all know keeping the ball deep—within about

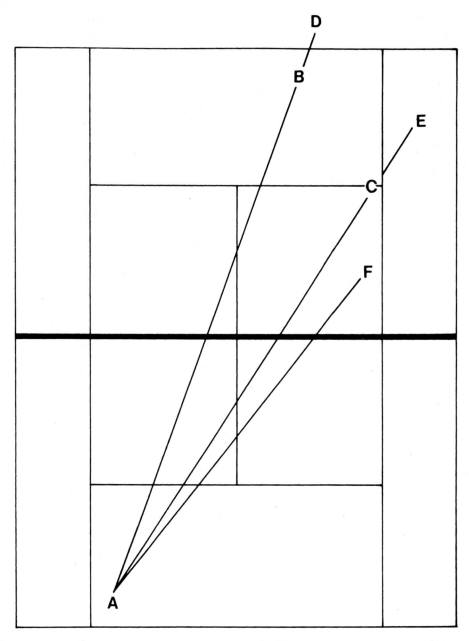

Topspin baseline drives and cross-court topspin passing shots

Chris Evert Lloyd about to play the cross-court topspin passing shot on the run.

four or five feet of the baseline—is the single most important tactic in baseline play because this prevents the opponent from suddenly taking the offensive and coming up to the net.

A ball containing topspin can comfortably clear the net before spinning back to earth. On the other hand, a flat shot struck with a good deal of pace runs a much greater risk of either catching the net or landing either long, D, or wide, E. If the shot is hit more conservatively, higher above the net and with less pace to keep it in, an opponent can more easily either put you on the defensive with an aggressive shot, or will have more time to run down any wider shot and return it more effectively.

Cross-Court Topspin Passing Shots

The cross-court passing shot is represented in the diagram by a line running from point A to point F. Passing shots are intended to laterally bypass your net-rushing opponent. There are two reasons for the greater difficulty of this highly angled shot. The first is attributable to the fact that the net becomes progressively higher toward its extremities, standing five and one-half inches higher at the juncture of the singles sideline than at the center. Second, there is less distance from A to F than from A to B or C. Nevertheless, this shot can actually be made fairly often by applying heavy topspin to force the ball down safely. This is a shot at which many of the top two-handers such as Evert Lloyd, Austin, Borg, and Solomon are remarkably adept. Solomon probably has the best cross-court topspin passing shot in tennis in recent years. I've seen him make it continually, even on the deal run, missing it only once or twice in an entire match. In addition, this shot is very difficult for the opponent to volley because it is dipping lower and lower as it comes over the net.

A flat passing shot hit along this same line of flight is more likely to remain airborne and sail wide. If it is hit a little more softly to keep it in, the opponent is afforded more time to intercept it and volley it aggressively. In order to avoid both the net and the doubles alley, the flat passing shot must more frequently be directed closer to the center where the net is lower. Unfortunately, a centrally placed shot is also easier to reach because the volleyer need not move so far. With the flat stylist's relative inability to hit the cross-court passing shot as consistently as the topspinner, he or she often comes to prefer the down-the-line shot. This is a Connors favorite. Next time you have a chance to observe him in action, make note of the ratio of down-the-line to cross-court passing shots he attempts. I think you will find that he not only prefers the former a little more than some of his peers, he is also a little more adept at it.

Topspin Approach Shots
An approach shot is hit after moving forward into the midcourt area in response to a weak shot that lands "short," in an area that extends roughly from just behind the service line all the way up to the net. As the diagram of approach shots shows, the down-the-line approach is to hit to a point B that is directly opposite the point at which the ball was played, and the cross-court approach is, of course, angled to the other side of the court, C. After stroking the approach shot, you can swiftly move up into the net position (forecourt) to volley. If you learn to hit your approaches on the run rather than stopping first, as some coaches advocate, you'll not only maintain better rhythm (a smooth flow in both movement and stroking that takes you from the midcourt to the forecourt), but also get into the net a bit more quickly.

Topspin, as always, will tend to force the ball down safely just inside the opponent's baseline or sideline. And as usual, a flat shot is more likely to sail out more frequently. Once again, if the shot is hit more softly, it will be much easier for the opponent to run it down and, in this case, hit a winning passing shot.

Topspin approach shots

APPROACHING DOWN THE LINE

Strategically speaking, most wider approach shots should be hit down the line because you can then move forward into the most advantageous net position in the least amount of time. Although primarily a baseliner, Harold Solomon is also the master of this shot. As you can see in the diagram, from this net position, X, you are best able to cover the full range of the opponent's possible passing shots as you bisect their angle. In other words, you'll be able to reach the widest shots hit to either side with equal quickness.

Notice also that a player positioned at point X is naturally closer to and "favoring" a passing shot directed down the line. Why? This shot has less distance to traverse before traveling past you than a cross-court shot. So, when assuming the net position, you must always be slightly closer to the down-the-line side of the court to allow yourself the time to intercept this quicker shot. And from this position, approximately three feet from the center line, with just one long stride, you can also reach all of the opponent's cross-court attempts except those that are perfectly placed just beyond your reach, but just inside the sideline. If your opponent is capable of making this demanding shot, you have no choice but to gracefully concede the point, perhaps offering a hearty "nice shot, friend." Remember though, on any given attempt the percentages are always in your favor that your opponent will either err or give you a shot at a volley. However, think twice about giving your two-handed foes too many opportunities to hit the cross-court passing shot. With their heightened potential to generate both topspin as well as acute angles, they are much more likely to make this shot on a higher percentage of attempts.

APPROACHING CROSS-COURT

If, on the other hand, you direct your approach shot cross-court, you are more likely to find yourself falling victim to a passing shot. As you can see in the diagram of approach shots, it takes longer to move from point A to point Z, which is equidistant from the opponent's most extremely angled possibilities, than from A to X. If you arrive at Z after the opponent has struck the ball, it will be difficult if not impossible to catch up with a shot heading down the line. Beware. Cross-court approaches are risky! Play the percentages and approach down the line most of the time. This is an honored, long-standing tenet that has served tennis players well, but which, I think, the two-hander can occasionally afford to bend a bit. Why?

Two-handed topspinners should be aware of the fact that since they have the capacity to hit the ball both harder and with tremendous angle, they can opt to approach cross-court sometimes, despite the risk. Against this angled rocket, it is doubtful that every opponent will have enough time to reach the ball and drill it back up the line for a placement. Or, if it can be reached, he or she may be intimidated into a very defensive posture by the very force of the shot. In choosing this tactic, there are several variables that you must consider: the speed of the opponent, the speed of the court surface (a court is said to be "slow" if its rougher, more abrasive surface tends to retard the speed of the bounce, and "fast" if its smoother surface does not reduce the speed so drastically), and his or her overall ability. Certainly the faster and more capable the opponent, the less likely you are to score with the cross-court approach. Connors, with his exceptional power, often wins points with this shot, and Andrea Jaegar likes this shot a lot, too.

Those of you who are right-handers, and that is roughly 90 percent of you, have the additional advantage of hitting two-handed backhands cross-court to the weaker backhands of your many one-handed opponents. If you really "rip" the approach he or she may be forced to hit late or otherwise respond with either a defensive lob or a weaker attempted passing shot, allowing you to quickly finish off the point at the net. It should behoove every right-handed two-hander to perfect this tactic. It will surely become invaluable through the years; you will have innumerable opportunities to incorporate it into your winning strategy. You must remember though, whenever you approach cross-court, you've got to really rifle the ball, or you may find yourself getting passed by either the weakest of opponents or the weakest of shots!

APPROACH SHOT EVENTUALITIES

The following are some other approach shot eventualities that you will find helpful and can blend into your own match play. They are based on the relative strength of your two-handed approach shot to the anticipated strength of the opponent's passing shot.

A highly angled, two-handed, right-handed forehand approach shot would normally be less effective when hit cross-court to another right-hander's forehand; it should most often be directed down the line to the backhand. You are then hitting the high percentage shot into your opponent's weakness. Against a leftie, however, this shot can occasionally be directed cross-court to attack the weaker backhand, just as the right-hander's backhand should usually be hit down the line to exploit this same left-handed backhand.

A left-handed, two-handed, cross-court backhand would also proceed to the right-hander's forehand. The leftie is, therefore, usually best off hitting down the line to the right-hander's backhand, saving the cross-court shot to take advantage of fellow left-hander's weaker one-handed backhands.

The left-hander's two-handed forehand approach would travel down the line to the right-hander's forehand and cross-court to the backhand, normally making the latter shot a wiser choice. However, the down-the-line shot would usually be the best alternative when facing the one-handed backhand of a brother or sister leftie. If you should happen to come upon the rare one-handed opponent with a backhand definitely stronger than the forehand, all of these directives may be reversed.

Approaching Against the Two-Hander

Not all of your opponents will be one-handers though, and as time passes, you will see more two-handers staring aggressively at you from across the net. How should you approach this matter of choosing the most effective approach shots to use against your more dangerous two-handed opponents? This can present a challenge, for if like most two-handers he or she has an offensive forehand as well as a potent two-handed backhand, there is no definite exploitable weakness. *Before* stepping out on the court, analyze your foe's game to determine which shot he or she is most capable of passing you with. More often than not, the two-hander will be the most lethal, so begin by approaching to the forehand side.

If you haven't had the opportunity to scout your two-handed opponent, or if you've determined that the respective shots are roughly equal in strength, then also start out the match attacking the forehand side. If you are getting passed too often after hitting what you consider forcing shots, then try approaching to the two-handed side. If you continue to meet with failure, you have the choice of staying back at the baseline or trying to produce even more aggressive shots while you continually "mix them up." That is, alternate your approaches in a random manner, to keep the opponent off balance and hard pressed to predict where you will strike next. If you don't vary your approaches, your opponent may begin to anticipate the direction of your shot and be positioned accordingly, thus depriving you, the aggressor, of much of your advantage.

The Open Court Beckons

One last word about approach shots: never ignore the open court. Regardless of the effectiveness of the shot you will hit and to which of the opponent's shots it is directed, if you can accurately hit the shot to the vacant area, you will win the point anyway.

THE TWO-HANDED TOPSPIN RETURN OF SERVE

The two-handed topspin return of serve is a very dangerous attacking weapon, the epitome of which is certainly the Connors backhand. The strength of the two-handed backhand return, in particular, constitutes one of the main areas of superiority over the one-handed game. Most two-handers actually favor this shot; consequently, their opponents are forced to serve to the forehand more often than they would against one-handers. Here once again, one encounters the dilemma of where to place the ball when facing the one-hander.

Connors, coiled and ready to throw himself at this return of serve.

On the other hand, against a strong serve, relatively few one-handers (below those at the upper levels) are capable of hitting an aggressive, forcing topspin backhand because again, as you will recall, this shot must be contacted so far out in front to be effective. Consequently, the size of the backswing will have to be severely reduced against a big serve. Typically then, many one-handers must be content to merely chip or slice their returns, utilizing the shorter backswing that accompanies these shots. (See the section in chapter 9 on "The Slice 'Chip' Return of Serve.") The strategy to follow against such players is no great mystery. You must attack the weaker backhand, directing nearly all of your deliveries there to draw as many weak, lethargic responses as possible. You can then pounce on these "sitters" with either a strong first volley or a forcing ground stroke or approach shot.

Returning Against the Serve and Volleyer

The aggressive two-handed topspin return of serve is particularly effective when opposing a player who likes to follow his or her serve into the net. The return can be made to drop very suddenly to the level of the net rusher's feet, forcing him or her to volley up defensively against this dipping, high-velocity projectile. Two-handers should always strive to use their greater potential for topspin to force the opponent to dig out those difficult low volleys. Or, the return can be angled so sharply that the server is unable to advance far enough forward to intercept it at all. The latter is the shot that kept Borg's opponents awake the night before their matches.

DOUBLES AND THE DOUBLE-HANDED GAME

Geoff Brown feels that the "return of serve really comes into its own in the game of doubles," (in J. Pollard [ed.], *Lawn Tennis the Australian Way*), in which returning well is so critical and in which you are also constantly faced with net rushing opponents. It isn't hard to see what Brown means if you are aware of the fact that all tennis experts stress that you must control the net to win in doubles. The two-hander can stand in closer and take the return on the rise (contacting the ball way out in front as it is still rising off the court) more effectively, with less chance of a fast serve dislodging his or her grip, and then advance into the net position more often and more quickly. Also in doubles, the wider court opens up more opportunities for acutely angled topspin shots placed just beyond the reach of the oncoming server. Combined with the two-hander's super volleying abil-ity (see chapter 11) and topspin lob potential (see chapter 8), the con-trolled power of the two-handed return of serve normally provides our hero with an overall edge in doubles.

You may remember that all three of the original "down under" boys, McGrath, Bromwich, and Brown, were doubles standouts. Unfortunately, our contemporary two-handed singles stars, with just a few exceptions (Evert Lloyd, Mayer, and Jaegar), rarely play dou-bles at all, mainly because they don't wish to expend the energy. In other words, they feel that by playing doubles they would jeopardize their chances of capturing the more lucrative and prestigious singles titles. While this is certainly understandable, from the spectators' point of view I think it rather unfortunate, because these stars have all the equipment to provide their legions of fans with a lot of great doubles action. How would you like to see the team of Borg and Connors in the finals of the U.S. Open or Wimbledon, or perhaps the team of Austin or Evert Lloyd? Great, huh? But, it's unlikely that we will see many of the top two-handers paired up too often, so don't get your hopes up too high.

Some would rightly contend that many top two-handers, for ex-ample, Borg, Austin, Evert Lloyd, and Jaegar, have developed win-ning singles games based almost exclusively on ground strokes that are simply so good that they have rarely had to attack the net. They have compiled tremendous winning records by just slugging it out from the baseline match after match, and tournament after tourna-ment. So, who needs to volley, right? In actuality, they are all much better volleyers than most television commentators give them credit for. For example, in the finals of the 1982 Australian Open, in which Chris Evert Lloyd defeated Martina Navratilova, she won seventeen of twenty-two points on which she approached the net. That's not bad for someone who supposedly "can't volley." The top two-hand-ers have not become even better volleyers, not through lack of talent but simply through lack of exposure to a tennis ball while in the fore-court. By playing more doubles, many two-handers could round out their singles games by cultivating the great volleying ability inherent in the two-handed method.

RETURNING AGAINST THE BASELINER

Against the baseliner, the two-hander can immediately get the oppo-nent "on the string" (pull him or her out of position) by hitting a highly angled topspin return which, if not an outright winner, may

Chris Evert Lloyd is a good volleyer despite what anyone says.

either force an error or possibly open the court for a winning placement on the next shot.

TWO-HANDED TOPSPIN LOBS AND MOONBALLS

A heavily topspun shot can be used to confuse or disturb your opponent. Such is the intention of the moonball. If you've ever seen Harold Solomon, Tracy Austin, or Andrea Jaegar play, you surely know how effective and disruptive it can be. They drive their opponents crazy with it!

With its tremendously arced trajectory, the moonball is the ultimate topspin shot. The excessive topspin, which causes the ball to drop, creating the radical trajectory, also causes the ball to bounce as high or even higher than the opponent's head. It is particularly difficult for the one-hander to deal with this shot on the weaker back-

When you see her high follow-
through and skyward look, you
know that Tracy Austin has just offered up one of her many moon-
balls.

hand side, and an opponent may ultimately succumb to frustration or fatigue when repeatedly forced to do so. You see, the moonball takes its toll mentally as well as physically.

Every two-hander should develop this shot because it is such a great change of pace from the typical low trajectory baseline drive, and it's easy to learn to pull off with the great topspin potential of two hands. You can use it either to force errors—winning some easy points with it outright—or to come into the net behind it and volley the opponent's weak response for a winner. You will also see Austin and Jaegar lofting them toward the heavens when they're pulled out of court by deep angled drives, buying priceless time in which to re-cover to the center. The moonball can be a "girl's best friend" dur-ing those tough baseline rallies.

An additional reason for acquiring this shot is that it automatically becomes a topspin lob when the opponent is up at the net. Here, the ball is lifted up quickly to the level just barely above the surprised net person's upwardly stretched racquet. The right amount of excessive topspin will force the ball to fall safely inside the baseline and bounce swiftly away from the pursuing opponent—going, going, gone!

DISADVANTAGES OF THE TOPSPIN GAME

As you might expect, the topspin style also has a few liabilities. Basically, they are the opposite qualities of the advantages of the flat game.

Maintaining Depth

Perhaps the biggest potential problem for every topspin player is maintaining sufficient depth of those ground strokes that are not intended to be highly angled. As mentioned, the more topspin that is applied to the ball, the greater is its tendency to descend quickly, landing short, and allowing an aggressive opponent to move forward quickly and possibly win the point by hitting a forcing approach shot or an outright winner. By delivering the short ball, the topspin stylist will be forced repeatedly into a defensive position, from which it is both difficult to hit passing shots and to win matches. At the beginning of his career, Bjorn Borg coughed up many more short balls than he now does. It was not until he acquired the ability to hit his heavily topspun drives with greater depth that he became the best player on the planet. Like Bjorn, if you intend to achieve as much as possible with the topspin style, you must constantly concentrate on keeping those arcing ground strokes close to your opponent's baseline.

Decreased Pace

The heavily topspun drive also lacks the sizzling pace of the flat shot because the path of the racquet is more vertical prior to impact, so that less direct force is applied to the ball. A shot with only moderate topspin contains more pace than a heavily topspun ball because the stroke used in producing it is more toward the horizontal plane. The path of the racquet head on a flat drive is the most horizontal, resulting in the most forceful application of power.

Higher Bounce

A heavily topspun ball will also tend to "sit up" for the opponent. This means that its bounce will be higher than that of a flat drive because it strikes the court at a more acute angle. Unless it is an extremely arced and super high-bounding moonball, the typical topspin drive will normally bounce to about waist height or just slightly

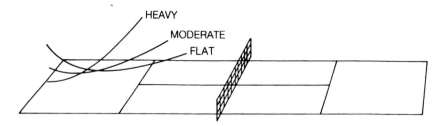

Topspin strokes
The path of the racquet head on a flat shot, a shot with moderate topspin, and a shot with heavy topspin

above it, which from the biomechanical viewpoint is the ideal height at which to stroke a tennis ball most efficiently.

Exhaustion
Another criticism occasionally leveled at the topspin game is that it is too exhausting. The assumption behind this accusation is that with the necessity to continually hit up so much, opposing the force of gravity, a player's energy would be depleted more quickly. It is true that the more vertical the stroke, the more energy is required to produce it, so that a topspin shot is naturally more enervating than a flat stroke. However, it is also true that a two-handed topspin player would be less likely to succumb to exhaustion than a one-handed player because with both sides of the upper body in operation, much less effort per stroke would be demanded. Fatigue would not occur as quickly if it were to occur at all.

THE FLAT VERSUS THE TOPSPIN STYLE

I sincerely hope that this analysis of the pros and cons of both styles of play will help you to gain a feeling for which is the most suitable for you. There is no question that both are worthy alternatives and that a serious student can, with a lot of joyful hard work, progress by cultivating either. However, I have always felt that the flat style is more difficult to master simply because there is so very little margin for error. I also believe that it requires many more years of training and practice to perfect it because it demands such precision. No doubt one of the reasons that Chris, Jimmy, and Tracy have done so is that they have been diligently working on it since each was below the age of six—and below the level of the net!

Jimmy Connors crunching another backhand; it's "take it to the limit" tennis every time he steps onto the court.

Powerhouse Tennis

That is not to say, though, that the flat style is not the most effective. When raised to its absolute height of perfection as it is when Connors is on the court, it is undoubtedly the ideal way to play the game. It is the ultimate in powerhouse tennis. Certainly, we have all fantasized about what it might be like to move from side to side, hitting the ball just as hard as we can, just a couple of inches above the net, for winner after winner. When he is at his best and truly on his game, as he was in 1982, he is virtually unbeatable. Unfortunately, not many others possess Connors's incredible timing, motor control, eyesight, and unyielding competitiveness, to say nothing of all those years of training and experience. Jimmy Connors is a unique player; he is remarkably consistent and successful with a style of play that few others could hope to employ so advantageously. For these reasons, the ever so exacting flat game is perhaps best suited to only the very finest athletes. As previously stated, the flat stylist often commits many

The high follow-through up and over the shoulder indicates that Chris Evert Lloyd has applied a little more topspin to this shot than she normally does.

more unforced errors. There will be days when even Jimmy will miss a greater number of shots than usual. This is the primary reason that Borg was once able to defeat him eleven times in a row.

High Marks for Topspin

Although the topspinner is the most consistent, he or she will normally not tally as many winning placements as the flatter hitter, and is less capable of continually placing the opponent on the defensive. Nevertheless, with all factors considered, we must conclude that the topspin style is slightly superior. With topspin, one is able to hit a greater variety of shots, including those that are acutely angled, which—when taken in sum—usually result in many fewer errors. This latter attribute is the most important consideration in ultimately evaluating the respective styles. For its steadiness we must grant high marks to topspin. Match play statistics invariably reveal that many more matches are lost by simply missing shots than are won by blasting winners. Consistency is of paramount value!

COMBINING STYLES

The very best two-handers are so skilled and highly trained that they are fully able to hit both flat and topspin shots equally well. Chris Evert Lloyd, Tracy Austin, and Andrea Jaegar, who together possess the most devastating ground-stroke attacks in women's tennis, are all basically flatter hitters. Their "groundies," during baseline rallies, normally contain relatively little topspin. Nevertheless, they are all adept at hitting the highly angled two-handed backhand passing shot, adding on lots of topspin to bring the ball down safely.

It is apparent that it is not necessary to adhere rigidly to one or the other of the extremes in style. They are merely outlines to which you may refer in order to mold a style that is best suited to your ideals and abilities. It is entirely possible to forge a game employing shots that contain an amount of spin anywhere along the continuum of spin that joins the two extremes. The degree to which your game is maximally offensive but also more error prone, as opposed to one which is somewhat less aggressive but also less error prone, will depend upon the ratio of flatter to topspin shots that you choose. "Choose" is the key word here. The ball is now in your court, the choice of style(s) is yours. So, let's begin to discover in detail the techniques used to produce the many different two-handed shots. You may then proceed in your adventure of defining your own two-handed style. We'll begin with two of the most fundamental and important components of all stroke production, first, grips, and second, footwork.

CHAPTER FIVE

GETTING A GRIP ON TWO-HANDED TENNIS

The positions of the hands, particularly the bottom or dominant hand, have important consequences for the two-handed ground strokes. The four major dominant hand grips are these: the eastern backhand, the eastern forehand, the western forehand, and lastly, the continental. Among the top two-handers, there is a good deal of variation in the grips used to hit the two-handed backhand. For instance, Bjorn Borg's right hand is placed in a classic eastern backhand grip. As you can see in the photo, much of the hand and wrist is positioned behind the racquet handle. The V that is formed by the thumb and index finger points directly at the left shoulder when the racquet is held directly out in front and perpendicular to the line of axis of the shoulders. Of course, the V would point toward the right shoulder of a left-hander adopting this grip. Jimmy Connors, a left-hander, prefers the eastern forehand grip, in which most of the hand and wrist is positioned in front of the handle so that the V points directly at Connors's left shoulder. A right-hander should have the V directed at the right shoulder. The western forehand grip is used by scrappy Harold Solomon. Notice that nearly all of the hand and wrist are positioned in front of the handle, and that the V is pointing toward the area outside the right-hander's shoulder. The continental grip is characterized by its neutral position. In other words, the hand is positioned neither in front of nor behind the handle, but rather above it, so that the V points at the player's center.

ADVANTAGES OF THE FOREHAND GRIPS

Almost all one-handed players learn to change from a forehand grip to a backhand grip to hit a backhand. On the other hand, the two-handed backhander need not change grips when alternating from forehand to backhand because the extra strength of the two-handed grip compensates for the weaker and less supportive frontal position of the dominant hand. This is one of the outstanding overall benefits of the two-handed game because it is desirable to eliminate grip

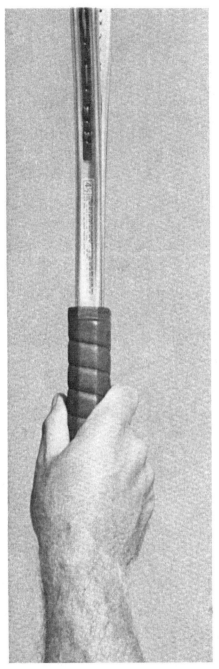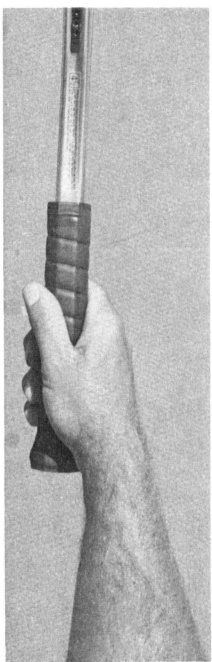

1. The eastern backhand dominant hand grip　　　2. The eastern forehand dominant hand grip

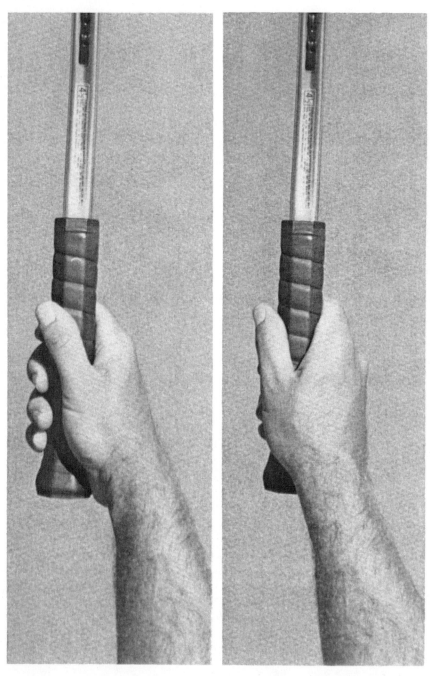

3. The western forehand dominant hand grip   **4.** The continental dominant hand grip

changes, whenever possible, in order to enhance stroke production through simplification. In other words, the less you attempt to do, the less there is that can go wrong!

Another advantage of both forehand grips is that they enable the dominant wrist to operate most efficiently to produce the greatest degree of leverage when hitting two-handed topspin backhands or forehands because the joint can move a slightly greater distance than when placed in the eastern backhand grip. To better comprehend this concept, you might try imagining the dominant hand working like a gate, swinging open and closed on its hinge, the wrist joint. Now, pick up a racquet and move it laterally back and forth with the wrist, using all four grips, and you will see what I mean. The western and eastern forehand permit more freedom of movement than the other two grips (although the continental is not far behind), and thereby enhance the power of the two-handed shots. The western grip actually permits the greatest amount of horizontal displacement, while this factor gradually decreases as you move the right hand counterclockwise through the eastern forehand and continental to the eastern backhand grip which allows the least movement. With greater displacement potential, the forehand grips also provide the greatest ease in deceptively changing the direction of any shot at the last moment. Gene Mayer uses his wrists to control the ball better than anyone else currently on the international scene. I'm sure that his opponents are convinced that there is an element of the magician in Gene. In chapter 8 we'll take a closer look at the importance of this wrist action in enabling you not only to fool an opponent but also to put a lot of extra topspin and zip on those two-handed drives, just like Borg and Solomon!

DISADVANTAGES OF THE FOREHAND GRIPS

The major disadvantage of both forehand grips is that they prove to be inadequate when one is forced to hit that occasional one-handed backhand. With so little of the hand and wrist behind the handle to support and strengthen the grip, it becomes quite difficult to hit the one-hander firmly. And with the face in such a naturally open position (inclined upward), it is virtually impossible to impart any topspin. A switch to the eastern backhand grip is a must if one is to hit a more aggressive shot. Despite the fact that this grip change violates the principle of maintaining the utmost simplicity in technique, it is not really a serious obstacle. For, with time and practice, almost everyone learns to make very rapid grip changes. It is a very rare occurrence when an experienced player is forced to hit any shot with an improper grip.

In choosing grips, you should be aware of the fact that with any forehand, the western makes it more difficult to play low balls, although it is easier to handle the high ones. Conversely, the high ones are more difficult to deal with using the eastern, while the low ones are easier.

ADVANTAGES OF THE EASTERN BACKHAND GRIP

One advantage of the eastern backhand grip is that it provides additional support on a two-handed backhand with the hand and wrist placed farther behind the handle. But all two-handed grips are inherently so strong and solid that this is only a minor plus. Another minor benefit concerns the fact that the hands fit most closely together when the dominant hand is in the backhand grip. The absolute proximity of the hands assures that they will work together more efficiently than they can when in the forehand grips, in which they are not so closely united. It is similar to the joining of the hands on a golf grip without the overlapping of the upper hand's index finger and the lower hand's "little pinky." Incidentally, I have noticed that most of the former one-handers who played with the eastern backhand grip retain this grip for their two-handed backhand when they make the transition to the two-handed style because it is just more natural for them. And then when forced to stroke one-handed on the backhand side, they are always best prepared for this eventuality. The capacity to hit every backhand without a grip change is the greatest advantage of the eastern backhand dominant-hand grip.

DISADVANTAGES OF THE EASTERN BACKHAND GRIP

The major disadvantage in using the eastern backhand dominant-hand grip is that it is not as conducive to the application of topspin or the use of deception because, as you know, the hands' lever action is somewhat restricted. A minor drawback is that it is a poor grip with which to hit any forehand because it naturally opens the face too much. So, here again, a grip change is necessitated. Bjorn Borg must change from the eastern backhand grip that he uses on his two-handed backhand to the western forehand grip to hit his long, looping one-handed forehand. This is a rather long way to go, but with training one can eventually learn to do it as rapidly and smoothly as Borg.

ADVANTAGES OF THE "NEUTRAL" CONTINENTAL GRIP

The continental grip is an adequate, indeed very popular, one-handed forehand grip. So, as is the case when using the forehand grips, it is unnecessary to switch grips when alternating between hitting one-handed forehands and two-handed backhands. The continental yields nearly as much leverage for topspin and deception as the forehand grips. Its primary advantage, though, is that it eliminates the need to change grips when hitting a volley following a ground stroke or another volley, because—as we shall discover in chapter 11—the continental is always the best grip to use at the net.

DISADVANTAGES OF THE CONTINENTAL GRIP

Unfortunately, like the forehand grips, the continental is also inadequate for hitting a one-handed backhand because the hand is more above and less behind the handle. It is, however, a bit closer to the backhand grip so that this grip change can be accomplished most quickly whenever it becomes necessary. And like the eastern, the continental is great for stroking the low ones, but not so good with the higher shots.

THE EASTERN FOREHAND OR CONTINENTAL NONDOMINANT HAND GRIP

With the dominant hand placed into any of the aforementioned positions, the nondominant hand, or upper hand, should be placed into an eastern forehand or continental grip. In this position, with the hand almost entirely behind the handle, maximum leverage for topspin and deception are guaranteed while maximum support is also applied. The nondominant hand should never be placed uncomfortably in front of the handle (the backhand position), because then both less leverage and less support are available. Regardless of the grips that you choose, the fingers of both hands should be spread comfortably along the handle, not bunched closely together as in a so-called "hammer grip." And both hands must squeeze the grip with an equal amount of pressure. In order to provide maximum support over the greatest area, the hands should not, like Eddie Dibbs's in the section on "The Open Stance" in chapter 6, be overlapped at all.

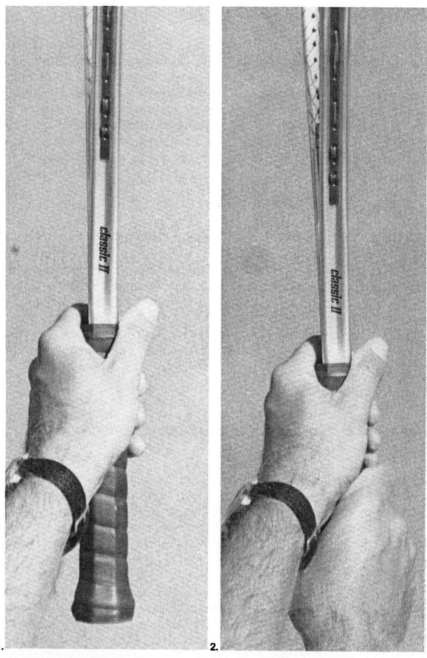

1. The continental is one of the two (along with the eastern) most popular and natural nondominant hand grips.
2. The best grip for the flat shot: the dominant hand in the eastern backhand position.

THE BEST GRIPS FOR THE TWO-HANDED BACKHAND

The Flat Style

Which is the best dominant hand grip to use on a two-handed backhand? I believe it depends upon the style of play that you wish to develop. If you want to learn to hit most of your shots with a minimal amount of topspin, I would recommend adopting the eastern backhand grip because the lever action of the wrists is less important on a flatter shot. In this position, the eastern backhand provides the most support for both one- and two-handed backhands.

The Topspin Style

If you lean toward the topspin style, I would advocate the adoption of either forehand grip or the continental. The wrists are critical to the production of heavier amounts of topspin as well as the facility to alter the direction of the shot, and should therefore be positioned to maximize the "wrist-snap" at impact. You might choose the grip you prefer for the one-handed forehand to eliminate having to switch grips to hit your two-handed backhand. In other words, for the sake of simplicity, don't place your dominant hand into an eastern forehand grip on your two-handed backhand, and then change to a western forehand grip for the forehand, or vice versa—switching from a western to an eastern. Likewise, if you have a continental forehand, retain this grip for the backhand. Try to use the same dominant-hand forehand grip for both shots.

ALTERNATIVES TO THE "BEST" GRIPS

It is also possible that you could successfully develop a flat or topspin game using just the opposite grips that I have recommended. After all, Bjorn Borg hits an excellent, deceptive topspin backhand with the dominant hand in an eastern backhand grip. Nevertheless, common sense dictates that most players opting for the topspin backhand would hit the shot harder and with more topspin and disguise by employing a forehand or continental grip. Likewise, you could also develop a sound flatter backhand using a forehand grip, as Connors does, but with less overall effectiveness in most cases.

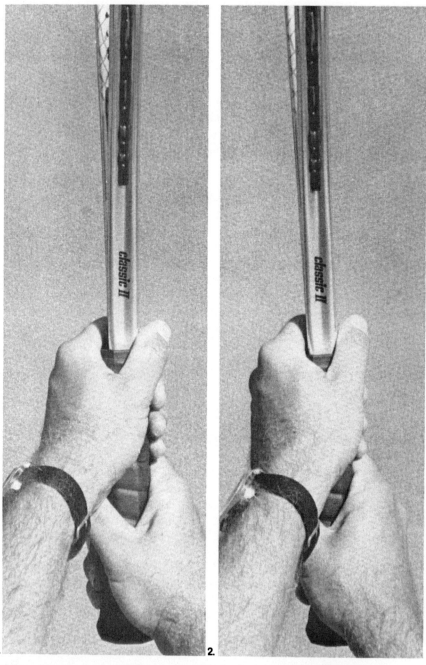

1. Two eastern forehand grips are the best combination for the dual two-handed topspin style.

2. Two continental grips are the best combination for the dual two-handed flat style.

THE BEST GRIPS FOR THE DUAL TWO-HANDED STYLE

The Topspin Grips
If you choose to go with two hands on both sides, I would nominate two eastern forehand grips as the best overall for the topspinner. The wrists would again be in nearly the ideal position for topspin and deception, and you'd always be prepared for a one-handed forehand. With the eastern as opposed to the western, you would sacrifice a bit of topspin potential but would not have to switch so far when hitting a one-handed backhand.

The Flat Grip
For the flatter hitters, I would advise the use of dual continental grips. The upper position of the hand is not a liability if you don't intend to utilize heavy topspin. The continental grip is, of course, adequate for hitting a one-handed forehand, and requires the least time to switch to a backhand grip when required.

THE BEST GRIPS FOR THE TWO-HANDED FOREHAND

The Topspin Grip
For that rare competitor opting for a two-handed forehand and a one-handed backhand, dual eastern forehand or dual continental grips (or combinations thereof) would provide plenty of topspin and disguise and would also allow you to hit a one-handed forehand without switching. Here again, the continental also puts you a little closer to the backhand grip than the eastern. The western would be advisable only if you want to consistently hit excessive topspin off your forehand.

The Flat Grip
If you wish to develop a flatter two-handed forehand, à la Pancho Segura, two continental grips would also clearly be the best alternative. Once again, it is an acceptable one-handed grip and would allow you to switch more quickly into an eastern backhand grip to hit your customary one-hander, than either forehand grip.

These are the best possible grip alternatives for *all* possible combinations of one- and two-handed styles of play, with the following two noteworthy exceptions.

The Nondominant Hand on the Bottom

It is also possible to reverse the positions of the hands for any two-handed shot by simply placing the dominant hand above the nondominant. Gene Mayer, Frew McMillan, and Hans Gildemeister all employ the so-called "cross-over" grip on both their two-handed forehands and backhands. After observing players who prefer this grip as well as those who place the dominant hand on the bottom, I have arrived at the following conclusions: With a cross-over grip, one is able to reach slightly farther on the forehand side, but can't reach quite as far on the backhand side. There is no appreciable difference in the quality of shots that can be produced with the respective grips; you can't hit it any harder or more accurately with one or the other. However, those who place the nondominant hand below are handicapped when forced to play a shot one-handed on either side. In such instances, they must attempt to perform a very tricky grip change; dropping the dominant hand down to the bottom of the grip to maximize their reach. But this is a much more difficult and time-consuming switch than that of simply changing from a forehand to a backhand grip, because the racquet handle must be moved in a vertical as well as a horizontal dimension. Unfortunately, with tennis being the high-paced game that it is, there may not always be time for this juggling act. Consequently, you will witness these players actually stabbing at shots with only a dominant hand positioned far up the handle in its normal two-handed grip position. This not only drastically limits one's reach, but also drastically reduces the centrifugal force, and hence, the power of any shot, by curtailing racquet head velocity. (A much less damaging difficulty concerns the need to switch grips after every serve to hit a two-handed ground stroke.)

The slight advantage of an increase in reach on the two-handed forehand is far outweighed by this grip's liability on all one-handed shots. With this significant liability, it is not surprising that the vast majority of two-handed players place the dominant hand below the nondominant. They are able to hit all of their shots just as effectively without ever having to make extremely awkward grip changes. And despite the success of the players that like to cross-over, I feel that most other two-handers should generally not be encouraged to try it. Only the fastest of the fastest two-handers can hope to excel with the cross-over grip.

Greg Holmes, the 1983 NCAA champ who recently turned pro, has devised an even more difficult approach to playing two-handed tennis. His system of grips is certainly the most complex and demanding in all of tennis. Greg hits his right-handed forehand with the left hand on the bottom and his backhand with the right hand on the bottom. Although this serves to maximize his two-handed reach, he is continually faced with the task of having to position the desired hand on the bottom of the handle. If, for instance, he has the right hand on the bottom and the ball is hit to the forehand side, he must make the quick juggle to get the left hand down below. Likewise, if the ball comes to the backhand side when his left hand is below, he is faced with the same tricky challenge. Thus Holmes is prone to be caught with the wrong grip or in between grips at the proverbial wrong time. In fact, he occasionally hits his forehand with his right hand on the bottom or his backhand with his left left on the bottom when there's no time to make the switch. He also tends to telegraph his expectations to the opponent concerning what shot he is expecting to have to hit on the return of serve, giving the server every opportunity to continually try to cross him up. And like the others with the cross-over forehand, Greg will occasionally be forced to hit wide one-handers with the right hand far up the handle.

Here again, despite Holmes's recent impressive ascension from the amateur to the professional ranks, I think most two-handers will get ahead in tennis far more quickly with the simplest, most efficient grip—the dominant hand on the bottom.

CHAPTER SIX

FOOTWORK AND THE TWO-HANDED GAME

Quickness of foot is a priceless attribute, especially for a two-handed tennis player. The top two-handers seem to be able to run down every ball! Likewise, precision in movement is also fundamental to optimal performance. There are two major positions or stances that one can adopt when stroking a tennis ball. One is termed the closed stance, and the other is the open stance. And as was the case with spins and grips, both stances have recognizable pros and cons.

THE CLOSED STANCE

Whenever a player is hitting from the closed stance, he or she is naturally positioned sideways to the net. In a perfectly positioned closed stance, it would be possible to draw an imaginary line through the toes that would extend to the area where the shot is headed. With this stance, one gains the greatest degree of equilibrium and is best able to transfer the weight onto the forward foot, just before impact, to maximize the force of the shot.

Whenever you are attempting to attack, and must hit a powerful, forcing shot, the closed stance should be utilized. Approach shots, most passing shots, and ground strokes hit during baseline exchanges in which you wish to assume or maintain the offensive, should all be hit most often out of the closed stance.

THE OPEN STANCE

In the open stance, one is either partially or completely facing the net at impact. Shots hit from this position are normally less potent because there is no leading foot for the body weight to move forward onto at impact and you can't use your thighs and hips as much to help accelerate the racquet head. The power of the one-handed backhand is diminished more than that of the forehand, being, as you will recall, less powerful to begin with. The backhand really depends on

The closed stance. A perfectly balanced Chris Evert Lloyd—"plant those feet and keep that head steady."

this forward weight transfer to realize its maximum power potential. Consequently, it is fairly common to observe the better one-handers hitting forehands from the open stance, but rarely if ever will you catch them hitting their backhands this way—by choice!

Conversely, two-handers are able to hit their backhands from the open stance without sacrificing nearly as much power. The additional wrist, arm, and shoulder provide enough extra impetus to compensate for the loss of power that results from not stepping into the ball, while the forehandedness and the more dynamic trunk rotation also bolster it. However, this stance is not recommended for use the majority of the time because it does not provide the natural weight transfer and related power of the closed stance. To compensate for the loss of natural power, a player hitting out of the open stance must "muscle" the ball to a certain extent. Harold Solomon and fellow American Eddie Dibbs, who has also been ranked in the world's top ten, can often be seen hitting their backhands facing the

Eddie Dibbs "muscling" the ball from the open stance.

net, with the weight on the back foot and the front foot up in the air. Although both are short in stature, they have very muscular upper bodies and legs. Personal power, coupled with the extra strength of two hands, enables them to hit the ball with tremendous velocity without any weight transfer. There can be no doubt, however, that less muscular specimens can hit the ball more offensively from the closed position, and should strive to do so most of the time.

Advantages of the Open Stance
Nevertheless, there are certain occasions when all two-handers can benefit by using the open stance. Certainly, the strength of the two-handed shot is most conducive to maximizing the advantages of the open stance. One of its principle benefits is that it is less time consuming; you can move back to the center of the court most quickly after playing a wide shot because you automatically make one less step prior to stroking. Consequently, one less step is then required in returning to the center to position yourself for the opponent's next

shot. You may say, "It is only one step, so what," but believe me, that one step can make the difference in being able to run down that next shot way over in the other corner.

The open position is also recognized for its deceptiveness. It is difficult to determine where the ball will be stroked because there is no leading foot and corresponding forward shoulder position to signal the direction of the shot. And the ball is naturally contacted 6 to 8 inches later from this stance—and the later it is met, the harder it is to discern its intended course. As a result, the opponent will have greater difficulty anticipating whether your passing shot will be heading down the line or cross-court. Remember though, what you gain in disguise with the open position, you may also lose in power. I suggest you put it to the test under match circumstances. If your are a relatively powerful two-hander, you may be able to get away with it. But if it turns out that the opponent has plenty of time to reach your passing shots and volley them effectively, then you should definitely start stepping into the ball to hit it harder.

The Open Stance on Slower Court Surfaces
The open stance is frequently seen on clay courts and other slow-playing surfaces upon which long baseline rallies normally occur. Here, pace is often less important than either the depth or the accuracy of shots because it is difficult to put the ball away when the opponent has so much time to reach it. The time-conserving open stance enables one to move most rapidly from side to side, retrieving the opponent's drives, keeping the ball in play and the opponent off the offensive until he or she either errs or allows you to take the offensive. If you intend to play a lot of clay court tennis, it would be especially wise to develop a two-handed topspin style to take full advantage of the open stance. You would then be able to position yourself most quickly and securely while retaining most of your full power as you battle to outsteady that opponent. You'd better hope his initials are not B.B., however. Bjorn Borg, the ultimate topspinner, is without a doubt the greatest clay court player ever. Many feel that in the years to come Mats Wilander is the only player with any chance of surpassing Bjorn's clay court preeminence.

The Open Stance on Faster Court Surfaces
The quicker bounce of the ball, off a faster court surface, affords you considerably less time to track it down. The open stance can be utilized here to maintain your position as close to the center as possible, and then cross the court in time to retrieve the next extremely wide shot.

Tracy Austin returning the high ball out of the open stance in the ad court.

The Open Stance on Return of Serve

Similarly, the two-hander can also employ the open stance advantageously on returns of serve. Jimmy Connors rarely hits two-handed backhands from the open position during a baseline rally. If he did, there is no way that he would generate the tremendous pace that results from a complete weight transfer. As you've no doubt observed, Connors really likes to lean forward into the shot, indeed hurls himself at it. However, he often hits backhand returns of serve from the deuce court out of the open stance. By holding his left foot back, he saves himself a step and gets to the center of the court just a little bit more quickly. Jimmy knows that it's essential to hastily recover to the center against a serve and volleyer because he'll be moving rapidly into the net with the intention of volleying the return away from Jimmy into the opposite corner. From the open stance, Connors has more time to cross the court and hit a passing shot or a topspin lob off of that first volley. On the other hand, if he returned

Jimmy Connors returning from the open stance in the deuce court.

from the closed position, he would arrive slightly later and might be left with no alternative but to lob defensively.

The Open Stance When "Jammed"

All tennis players, be they one-handed or two-handed, are frequently obliged to return from the open stance whenever a bullet is directed right at their bodies. It is necessary to quickly step sideways, out of the way of the ball, and there often simply isn't enough time available then to step forward onto the leading foot to recover one's balance. Whenever a smart opponent jams you like this, whether it is on a serve, a volley, or an overhead smash, it is difficult to respond with a forceful shot because you are unable to extend your arms at impact. You experience that "scrunched-up" feeling. Fortunately, as a two-hander you're less likely to be completely overpowered by these intimidating shots, with your capacity to muscle the ball when necessary.

Connors has that "scrunched-up" feeling on this return of serve from the ad court.

Returning Against the Baseliner

When competing against those who prefer to trade strokes, try to return from the closed stance as often as possible. With the opponent at the baseline, you will have a bit more time to reach the center before he or she plays your return, so the more time-consuming closed stance should not be a hindrance. And with the more potent stance, you'll be able to place the ball deeper into the opponent's court most consistently, and with maximum pace.

COMBINING STANCES

As situations continually change during the course of a tennis match, as an offensive position gives way to a defensive one and vice versa, a well-rounded two-hander must be able to alternate smoothly between the two positions to capitalize fully on the distinct advantages of

Perfect footwork has brought Tracy Austin into just the right position to step forward into this backhand.

each. I recommend that for every shot you learn, you first work toward acquiring the more fundamental and powerful closed stance and then afterward begin experimenting with the more economical and deceptive open position.

SHORT, QUICK LITTLE STEPS

The next time that you have the pleasure of watching either Jimmy Connors or Tracy Austin perform, notice how they move into position with very short, mincing steps. It's not unexpected to find that their footwork is just as precise as their stroke production. In fact, Jimmy and Tracy probably have the best footwork in tennis for a two-handed male and female, respectively.

Mincing is not only the fastest way to cover the relatively short distances that tennis demands, but is also the most precise way to position yourself just the correct distance from the ball. It's interesting to note that Dr. Groppel's studies also revealed that two-handers contact the ball the same distance from their bodies as one-handers when they are able to position themselves comfortably without lunging. To attain efficient positioning, observe the following guidelines: do not permit your elbows to rub against your stomach, impeding the acceleration of your arms and racquet. Similarly, at impact make certain that the arm connected to the anterior shoulder is virtually straight, but not locked, on all two-handed shots. This assures that the racquet travels its maximum arc to maximize its acceleration. Of course, this is not always possible if you're jammed, for instance, but it's something you should continually strive for. Conversely, try not to be so far from the ball that you must lunge for it. With a little practice, you will readily discover that comfortable distance/position that is just right for you.

With those supergrooved strokes, Tracy Austin is still in control when on the run.

BALANCE

And now, a last word about a factor that is very important on any and all shots—balance. You must attempt not to run through your ground strokes, but rather stop or at least retard your momentum as much as possible. Allow your head to be your focal point of this experience of equilibrium. If your head remains virtually motionless, on the horizontal dimension (side to side, not up and down), you are likely to be on balance. By stabilizing yourself as much as possible just before, during, and after the moment of impact, you provide the racquet with the smoothest and most unerring path to its target. This is an essential ingredient of the technical philosophy of Chris Evert Lloyd's original coach—her father, Jimmy Evert. In her autobiography (*Chrissie: My Own Story*, New York: Simon & Schuster, 1982), Chris confides that as a youngster she was taught that "if you keep your head absolutely motionless and your feet solidly based on the court, you could do anything with a tennis ball." Obviously, this degree of balance is not always attainable; many shots must be played on the dead run, but again it's something to shoot for constantly. When you have developed powerful and reliably grooved two-handed strokes, though, you will be able to compensate for much of the relative imbalance that naturally results from hitting on the run.

In the next three chapters we will discuss in detail how to hit the flat shot, the topspin shot, and lastly one we have yet to consider fully—the slice shot.

CHAPTER SEVEN

HOW TO HIT THE FLAT TWO-HANDED GROUND STROKES

As with all shots in the game, the stroke used in producing the flat shot can best be defined by its backswing and follow-through. The specific techniques for hitting both the flat two-handed forehand as well as the backhand are essentially identical, so the following stroke production analysis applies equally to both. The only significant difference is that for the forehand you must push with the dominant arm and pull with the nondominant arm, while these roles will be reversed on the backhand.

THE READY POSITION

The flat shot, like every shot, is initiated from the "ready position," so called because if you're in it—you are! In other words, from this position you'll be able to get the racquet back immediately and then move to the ball and position yourself most quickly. As you can see in the photo sequence of the flat shot, the racquet is held well out in front of the body and the head of the racquet is elevated above the hands. The knees are bent to facilitate a rapid lateral or forward movement, and the weight is held somewhat forward so that you are on the balls (the forward third) of your feet, *not* your heels. It is important to always be on your toes so as to be able to start moving to the ball immediately. You will discover that when you're caught back on your heels that you just can't get going. It's kind of like playing tennis in slow motion!

THE BACKSWING

To hit any type of shot, you should first turn your shoulders fully in order to take the racquet back into the hitting position as soon as you know to which side the ball is heading. At the completion of the backswing, the racquet should be pointing toward an area slightly behind and in back of your rear shoulder *as* you're moving to the ball, and the wrists should be slightly laid back (angled) so that they are in the firmest, most stable position. The racquet head will also travel slightly farther with the wrists laid back, providing it with additional momentum.

It is important to note that the extra strength of two hands allows the double-hander to lay the wrists back a little farther without making the stroke so long that the ball will be contacted late. Many one-handers, however, are prone to lay the wrist back so far that they can't bring the racquet through on time, and find it particularly difficult to hit cross-court.

At the completion of the backswing, on any two-handed shot, the posterior arm must be bent anywhere from approximately 20 degrees to nearly 45 degrees—depending on the type of preparation that is used. (See the section in chapter 10 on "The Semielliptical Backswing.") This arm must straighten toward impact to increase the leverage and thus the power of the two-hander. Whenever I have a student who just can't seem to generate any power, the first thing I look for is a straight and stiff posterior arm. In such cases, it is usually unnecessary to look any further for the problem.

To repeat: As on every shot, if you don't train yourself to begin the backswing immediately upon determining to which side the ball is directed, you may unfortunately also hit the ball late. Observe the top players: invariably there is never any hesitation. The importance of early preparation can never be overemphasized!

CLOSING THE STANCE

As you take the racquet back, you should step forward onto your leading foot to close your stance and place yourself sideways to the net. For both the right-handed, two-handed backhand and the two-handed, left-handed forehand, you should step onto the right foot. To hit both a right-handed, two-handed forehand and a left-handed, two-handed backhand, you should advance the left foot.

Generally speaking, the longer the stroke, the longer must be the forward step. With the slightly shorter radius (follow-through) of the two-handed shot, the step needs to be a little shorter than that of the one-hander, also serving to shorten the time it takes to set up for the two-hander.

The flat shot, hit in this case with a semielliptical backswing

1. The ready position.
2. The shoulders begin to turn immediately as the racquet is taken back.
3. At the completion of the takeaway, the racquet head is slightly below the point of contact.
4. The racquet head begins its acceleration to the ball as the front foot comes forward to close the stance.

3.

4.

7.

8.

5. The racquet head has dropped down and is beginning its approach to contact from just beneath the intended point of impact.

6. The wrists are firm as the ball is contacted just in front of the forward foot.

7. The racquet proceeds through the hitting area as the hips and shoulders rotate and the weight comes forward with the knees bent.

8. Here is the long and relatively low follow-through that characterizes the flatter shot. The racquet is pointing slightly upward, to an area just above the target.

THE NEARLY FLAT STROKE

The exact height of each backswing will naturally vary with the height of every ball. The key is to approach balls that are below the level of the net from a point that is *just beneath* the level of the anticipated contact point. You are then able to hit *upward slightly*, in order to drive the ball up and over the net. If, however, you approach the ball on exactly the same level, without lifting up at all, it will travel straight into the net. Such a perfectly flat drive, the result of a perfectly flat stroke, should not be utilized; it is destined to fail. Rather, the racquet should be guided forward along a nearly horizontal, but not absolutely horizontal path. With this slight upward stroking angle, the so-called flat shot will actually contain some small amount of topspin. It is possible to approach higher balls, those that are already above net level, with a perfectly horizontal stroke and still clear the net while imparting an indistinguishable degree of forward rotation.

THE "ROLE" OF THE WRISTS

On a flat shot, the wrists should remain quite a bit firmer, throughout the stroke, than on a topspin shot. This is due principally to their lack of contribution to the production of greater amounts of topspin. They can, however, be used to alter the direction of the shot, just as they can on a shot containing more topspin. But with less of a tendency to use the wrists on the flatter shots, the flatter hitters don't seem to learn to use their wrists for this purpose as often or as skillfully as someone like Borg or Mayer.

If the wrists are relatively firm as the racquet goes back, they will keep the racquet head up on the higher level appropriate to a flatter shot. Be sure to keep them quite firm at impact (unless being used for disguise) and your contact with the ball will be nice and solid.

CONTACT AND HORIZONTAL EXTENSION

The ball should meet the strings a few inches in front of the leading foot; perhaps slightly farther in front than the desired contact point on a topspin shot. This extra margin of forward contact naturally produces the longer and more horizontally extended movement that defines the topspin stroke. Jimmy Connors's well-known tendency to take the ball way out in front and on the rise is certainly facilitated

Caress those two-handers—as does Tracy Austin. Hold that ball on the strings!

by the use of the flat stroke. (With any ground stroke, regardless of style, it is always important to be aggressive, to go after the ball— not let it come to you. Try not to back up unless forced to by a very deep shot.) At contact, on both the flat and topspin shots the racquet head should be just above the level of the hands, so that the racquet itself is at a very slight upward angle.

HITTING THROUGH THE BALL

The term *hitting through the ball* refers to the continuous motion which produces a smooth forward flow from the end of the back-swing all the way to the end of the follow-through, allowing the strings to remain in contact with the ball for as long as possible. It may appear to the naked eye that the ball hits and leaves the strings immediately. However, research demonstrates that the sphere actu-

1. The author is simulating hitting the one-handed forehand with the nondominant arm. The feeling here is that of pushing.
2. The author is simulating hitting the one-handed backhand with the nondominant arm. The feeling here is that of pulling.

ally remains in contact for a fraction of a second; it is very important to realize that the longer you can "carry" the ball forward on the strings, the greater is the amount of control you will exercise over it. Remember though, the ball should not be allowed to move up, down, or sideways on the strings too much during contact. If it does, it will contain too much spin to be properly classified as a flat shot.

THE PUSH-AND-PULL ALLIANCE

On any two-handed backhand, you should always consciously attempt to bring the racquet forward with a feeling that the dominant hand, arm, and shoulder are pulling and that the nondominant side components are pushing. *The nondominant side should actually do a slightly greater percentage of the total work to fully capitalize on its powerful forehandlike action. On any two-handed forehand, the roles of the arms are naturally reversed; the dominant side will push and work a bit harder in supplying the sum power of the shot, while the nondominant side pulls.* On any two-handed shot, it is essential to make the arms operate as a single functioning interdependent unit and not as independent agents working at cross purposes. Specifically, both arms should be nearly straight (but not locked) immediately after impact and should then bend approximately the same amount, simultaneously, as the racquet proceeds to the follow-through. The elbows will then be comfortably positioned about 12 inches apart.

Try to be particularly conscious of the role played by the nondominant arm on any two-handed shot regardless of style. If you seem to be having difficulty pushing enough with this previously untrained member on the backhand, you might try the following learning techniques. Imagine yourself to be hitting a one-handed forehand with the nondominant arm as you stroke your backhand. Or, with the nondominant hand in its two-handed grip position, up near the handle, attempt to actually hit some slow-moving balls with what amounts to a nondominant arm forehand.

If you are having some difficulty utilizing the nondominant arm on the two-handed forehand, there is a similar, although slightly more difficult exercise you can use. With the hand positioned up the grip, attempt to stroke some nondominant arm one-handed backhands in order to get the feel for what it is like to pull more on this shot.

HIPS, SHOULDERS, AND KNEES

As you contact the ball, your shoulders and hips should turn smoothly in unison. The lower the ball, the lower you must bend in order to see it clearly. But most importantly, the knee bend allows you to transfer your weight into the shot, while retaining your balance. If your legs remain straight, with the knees locked, the weight cannot flow forward, increasing the amount of work the upper body must do to create the power. At impact, nearly all of your body weight—let us say about 90 percent—should flow forward and be supported by your front foot. This rotary action of the trunk produces a transfer of power upward from the knees to the thighs and hips, and into the trunk and shoulders; one action catalyzes the next as power is released through the arms at impact in a total summation of force. Naturally, with the lesser degree of vertical lift of a flatter shot, this lifting action is less than that which occurs during a topspin shot. More of the weight will go more directly outward toward the target. Here again, Jimmy Connors provides a great illustration of what it's like to really lean into the ball.

Jimmy Connors demonstrates the longer follow-through that characterizes the flatter stroke.

A few words of caution: always be certain that you are actually bending from the knees and not from the waist. Many players experience a false sense of ''getting down'' when bending over from the middle.

THE FOLLOW-THROUGH

The completed follow-through should be long and relatively low on a flat shot; lower than a topspin follow-through. However, a follow-through that is too short will normally indicate that the racquet head was slowing down at impact rather than *accelerating* as it must. When you finish correctly on this shot, your arms will be only slightly bent with the hands at about the same height as your head.

One thing to watch out for with the greater torso rotation of the two-handed stroke is the tendency to pull the racquet around or across the body instead of allowing it to go up and outward toward the target. The racquet head should actually move a little bit *inside out*, meaning that it should travel progressively farther away from the body as it gets closer to the ball. After impact, you should allow the racquet to move along the exact line of the ball's flight to increase accuracy of placement. To further assure that your stroke is "true" in this regard, feel the palm of the hand that is behind the handle go in this direction also. If the racquet deviates from this path and is pulled off the line of the ball's intended flight, you will inadvertently introduce an unwanted new direction to the shot.

CHAPTER EIGHT

HOW TO HIT THE TWO-HANDED TOPSPIN GROUND STROKES

In chapter 4, we discussed the phenomenon of topspin and reviewed the various properties that make it so valuable and therefore omnipresent on tennis courts the world over. Now, before analyzing the techniques used in hitting the various topspin shots, I would like to describe briefly how topspin is produced so that I may clear up some common misunderstandings.

THE ANGLE OF THE FACE AND THE PATH OF THE STROKE

Topspin is created by hitting upward *through* the ball. The greater the vertical distance the racquet moves prior to impact, the more topspin can be generated. It makes sense then, that if you are to hit up forcefully to the ball, the racquet face cannot be too open (inclined upward) if the ball is not to sail beyond the length of the court. Rather, the racquet face must be approximately perpendicular to the court at impact to allow the ball to roll down the strings and leave with a rapid forward rotation.

The angle or setting of the face, in conjunction with the path of the stroke, will determine both the height and depth of each shot. Generally speaking, if the racquet face is roughly perpendicular, then the more vertical the stroke, the higher above the net the ball will pass, but the shorter in the opponent's court it will land. If carried to its extreme, the stroke can become so vertical that the ball will contain so much topspin that it will not even travel as far as the net. Therefore, the player employing topspin must, for every shot, continually choose the correct racquet face angle and a stroke with just the right velocity and vertical path to produce a shot with just the desired trajectory. This all sounds tremendously complex and difficult, but with training, the preparatory wrist movements that establish the correct angle of the racquet face, as well as the upper body and arm movements for executing any topspin shot, become quite automatic.

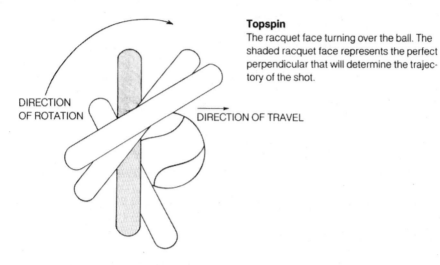

Topspin
The racquet face turning over the ball. The shaded racquet face represents the perfect perpendicular that will determine the trajectory of the shot.

DIRECTION OF ROTATION

DIRECTION OF TRAVEL

TURNING THE RACQUET FACE OVER THE BALL

Although it is natural to roll or turn the racquet face over the ball a little bit on any topspin shot after it has left the strings, it is a misconception to believe that the racquet must be radically rolled over to create heavy topspin. Actually, topspin can be generated with or without this technique.

What actually occurs here is a slight opening of the face on the backswing and a progressive closing (inclining downward) of the face toward impact, serving to increase racquet head torque and culminating in faster forward ball rotation. After impact the face continues to close—turn over—but during that brief fraction of a second of impact it is straight up and down.

Despite the fact that two-handers possess maximum racquet head control and can therefore be observed using this technique more than one-handers, it takes time to gain precision with it because it demands flawless timing. You must be able to meet the ball exactly as the face arrives at the perfect perpendicular angle to give the shot just the desired trajectory. If the face is just a tiny bit more open than 90 degrees, insufficient topspin will be applied and the ball is likely to travel long or wide. If the face is a bit too closed, the ball may catch the net or land much too short in the court.

It is considerably safer to apply topspin without this risky wrist action: instead of trying to adjust the face as it is contacting the ball, simply set it at the desired angle as it begins its forward/vertical movement, maintaining it there until after the ball has departed the strings. After you have correctly positioned the racquet at the perpendicular, firm up your wrists enough so as not to lose this "setting." This means that the wrists should rotate neither clockwise very much for shots on the left side of the body, nor counterclockwise, for shots on the right side.

THOSE SWEDISH WRISTS

Despite the greater difficulty involved in turning the face over the ball and maintaining control, there are several well-known two-handed professionals who have become quite successful with the technique, Bjorn Borg being the most notable example. With his extraordinary athletic ability, he has been able to perfect it and has thus substantially increased the amount of topspin at his disposal. However, most others who are not as gifted or highly trained as the Swede will have considerably more difficulty mastering it, and should re-

Those Swedish wrists are ready to roll!

strict its use to those few shots that must have excessive topspin—the moonball and the topspin lob. I think that you will find that you can obtain the degree of topspin that you need for all your other shots without resorting to turning the face way over the ball. We'll say more about this technique later in the chapter for the benefit of the more daring souls with those "Swedish wrists."

TOPSPIN TECHNIQUES

As before with the flat strokes, this analysis applies to both the two-handed forehand and backhand, as the techniques are identical. See the photo sequence of the topspin shots for additional information.

The Backswing

From the ready position, turn your shoulders to take the racquet back into a lowered hitting position. To impart substantial topspin, the racquet must approach the ball from *at least a foot or so* below the point of contact. The greater the distance below the point of contact from which the racquet begins its upward motion, the greater is the amount of topspin that can be imparted. Some two-handers like to drop the racquet head itself *slightly* below their hands at the completion of the backswing to get even further beneath the ball. This can be accomplished by simply relaxing the wrist muscles a bit—but only a bit, because if you loosen them too much the head will drop so

The wrists are laid back and the face is slightly closed at the end of the backswing for the top-spin shot.

The topspin shot, hit in this case with a straight-back backswing

1. The ready position

2. The shoulders turn immediately to begin the takeaway

3. At the completion of the takeaway, the racquet head is well below the point of contact. The front foot has stepped forward to close the stance.

4. The racquet approaches the ball from well below the point of contact in order to brush up the back of the ball and apply topspin.

5. The ball is contacted just ahead of the forward foot.

6.,7. The racquet proceeds up and through the hitting area as the hips and shoulders rotate and the weight comes forward with the knees bent.

8. The elbows begin to bend in unison as the racquet head passes up above the nondominant side shoulder into its customary high topspin follow-through position.

Topspin

The racquet head is "brushing" the ball as it rolls down the strings and leaves with your friend and mine—topspin.

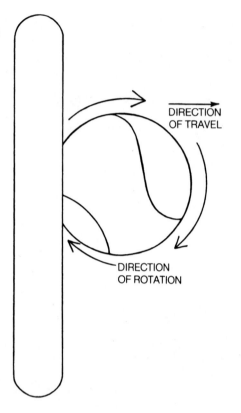

DIRECTION OF TRAVEL

DIRECTION OF ROTATION

low that even a two-hander won't be able to control it. And bending your knees a little bit more will also help you to approach the ball from well beneath—whether you drop the racquet or not. As with the flat shot, the wrists should again be laid back to stabilize and lengthen out the stroke. The topspinner, though, will normally lay them back a bit more than the flatter hitter in order to produce more topspin. And at the completion of the backswing, the face should be slightly closed. If this wrist position is not altered and the angle of the face is maintained, the face will be properly vertical at impact. As the racquet is going back, get sideways to the net by stepping onto the front foot. Remember, later work on stroking from the open stance.

Pushing and Pulling Vertically

As always, you should consciously attempt to both push as well as pull with the respective arms. In the case of the topspin shot, though, you must push and pull in a more vertical direction.

Contact

Once again the ball should be contacted even with or slightly in front of the forward foot. It need not, however, be met quite as far forward as a flat shot in order to create the more vertically extended movement that produces topspin.

Brushing the Ball

As the diagram shows, allow the ball to roll down the strings as the racquet head proceeds up and through the hitting area into its high finishing position. Another way of describing this action is to say that the face must be pulled up the back of the ball, "brushing it." This long contact permits the ball to pass across a maximum number of strings. (Even though you know that the ball resides on the strings only momentarily, consciously try to "hold" the ball for as long as possible—it *will* increase control.)

Hips, Shoulders, and Knees

At impact, the hips and shoulders should turn smoothly in unison with the knees bent. With the upward momentum of the topspin stroke, there will be a much greater natural tendency to rise up and straighten the knees as the upward thrust of the thighs and hips propel (accelerate) the racquet head up and through the ball by catalyzing the rotation of the trunk and shoulders. As you experience this feeling of rising up and through the contact point to the follow-through—as opposed to "staying down" as some teachers recommend—try to keep your head steady and avoid lunging. Remember, a smooth two-handed synchronization of movements is the most effective.

Flexing the Elbows and Following Through

After driving up and through the ball, the forearms should then be flexed, or pulled upward in unison. Their ascension from the elbows serves to further increase the vertical progress of the racquet. This flexing action also assures that the follow-through will be very high, as it must to produce topspin. The racquet head should finish just *above* the opposite shoulder; feel your posterior shoulder touch the bottom of your chin and you'll know you've made the proper high topspin follow-through. Incidentally, I feel it's best to keep both hands on the handle all the way to the completion of the stroke for ease and smoothness of preparation. In other words, you won't be able to get the racquet back into the hitting position as quickly on the following backswing (or two-handed forehand) if you release your nondominant hand. Bjorn Borg and Harold Solomon are the only

Rodney Harmon, an up-and-coming two-hander out of Southern Methodist University, is rising up off the court in applying topspin to this return at the U.S. Open.

major two-handers who consistently let go prior to completing their follow-through. However, those who contend that they don't hit true two-handers are mistaken: A shot can be accurately classified as a two-hander when both hands are on the handle at impact, in close proximity, and the posterior arm and shoulder function in a forehandlike manner. In light of these criteria, the traditional use of the nondominant hand on the throat of the racquet to assist in the backswing for a one-handed backhand does in no way constitute two-handed stroke production.

The Wrists and the Two-Handed Shots
Laying the wrists back also puts them in position to be snapped. The more they're laid back and also dropped, the more dramatically they can be snapped. Most successful players—be they one-handed or two-handed—begin to use greater degrees of wrist flexion after they have mastered the initial fundamentals of stroking. In actuality, the

Bjorn Borg has let go in completing this extremely high topspin follow-through, but rest assured that this is still a true two-hander.

better the player you become, the more you can effectively utilize the wrists. The wrists not only provide extra power, but as flexible joints they play a pivotal role in determining direction by orienting the face at impact. Of course, certain authorities fear that the use of the wrists is detrimental to stroke production. For instance, Vic Braden contends that Jimmy Connors—with the firmest wrists in the game— has the utmost control. Although this appeals to one's common sense and sounds very good in theory, it is something that is very difficult to substantiate. After all, Borg and Mayer can hit the ball on a dime with a lot of wristiness. I think, perhaps, that Vic's advice is directed primarily to one-handers.

At any rate, as many two-handed topspinners can attest, a rapid forward and upward flexion of the wrists adds an entirely new dimension to hitting a tennis ball. The vertical progress of the racquet head brushing up the back of the ball is accelerated to increase both the amount of topspin as well as the pace that may be applied to the

American teenager and ATP pro
Jimmy Brown has really dropped
the racquet head to brush up and
over this ball to apply topspin.

shot. This is an extremely important technique and certainly marks one of the main points of departure between one- and two-handed styles of play. The intensity of a highly controlled, yet powerful wrist snap is an experience that most one-handers will never know. The one-hander is always correctly admonished to keep the wrist firm to maintain control of the racquet head, but not the stronger two-handed topspinner; this dynamic action is ever so critical to his or her style. Check out the picture of Jimmy Brown: see how low and laid back his wrists are.

Deception and the Use of the Wrists

Furthermore, these wristy shots are the easiest to disguise successfully. By delaying the wrist snap until the last possible instant, the ball can be deceptively pulled cross-court when it appeared that it would be hit down the line. Whenever you hear anyone discussing Borg's or Solomon's backhands, or any of Mayer's shots, they al-

Gene Mayer has used a lot of wristiness to hit this forehand "on a dime."

most always make a remark such as: "You can't 'read it', so you never know exactly where it's going until after it has left the strings." This gives the two-hander a tremendous advantage especially when attempting a passing shot. Many a net-rushing opponent has been caught going the wrong way with an embarrassed expression after vainly trying to guess where the two-hander's shot is heading.

Power and Deception
Although the two-handed backhander gains some natural disguise by taking the ball a little farther back to begin with, his or her potential for disguise is also enhanced by the ability to hit the ball even later (relative to the normal contact point) without losing much power. On the other hand, the one-hander will normally lose considerable power when hitting the ball late (relative to the standard more forward contact point) because the racquet will not have traveled a sufficient distance prior to impact. Unlike the two-hander, though, the

Gene Mayer will hit this two-handed forehand a little late but won't lose much power with both hands on the racquet. Notice the "cross-over grip" with Gene's left (nondominant) hand on the bottom.

one-hander does not have the additional strength to compensate for this lack of momentum. The farther in front the ball is met, the easier it is for the opponent to detect its intended course; the later it is contacted, the more difficult the shot is to anticipate. Consequently, the two-hander can completely fool an opponent by slightly retarding the snap of the wrists and taking the ball later, while sacrificing relatively little of the power that a passing shot requires.

The Open Stance and the Wrists

With the ability to take the ball later and use the wrists in such a deceptive manner and still stroke the ball powerfully from the equally deceptive open stance, where, as you will recall, the ball is taken later naturally, two-handers have an extraordinary capacity to cloak their passing shots. The most difficult shot in the tennis world to anticipate has to be a two-handed topspin backhand passing shot, hit with a lot of wrist action, from the open stance. Where is the shot going? Only the wrists know for sure!

The Excessively Topspun Shots

The passing shot, the approach shot, the moonball, and the topspin lob can all be most proficiently executed using the wristy two-handed topspin stroke. Although they are all hit with the same basic technique, the latter two require more topspin hence wrist snap. But be careful here; everyone has their limits. Initially, you don't want to try to use so much wrist that you sacrifice all control over the racquet head. As you become more adept with this special tool, you can gradually employ more and more wristiness to your advantage.

The Topspin Passing Shots and Approach Shots   In the photo sequence of the excessively topspun shot, I am demonstrating the basic technique used in producing heavy topspin, in this case for an angled passing shot or approach shot. The racquet head must approach the ball from *well beneath* the point of contact. The finish is of equal importance in creating topspin. A very abrupt stroke, one lacking horizontal extension and coupled with a very high follow-through, will also help you maximize topspin.

The Moonball and the Topspin Lob   The moonball and topspin lob are executed in much the same manner but require an even greater amount of wristy topspin because they must be brought down suddenly from a much greater height (by the term *lob* is meant a relaxed, high-arcing shot). Consequently, the backswing must be even lower than for a passing shot; the racquet must almost touch the court. And the stroke itself must be even more vertical and abrupt, with the racquet passing well *over* the opposite shoulder and almost touching the back. It is also helpful to lean back with the upper torso to get under the ball more to lift it up quickly (although this backward rocking action reveals your intention).

"Let the Good Times Roll"

Now, as promised, let's talk about excessive topspin again. To increase the amount you can apply to the moonball and topped lob, experiment by attempting to roll the racquet face *over* the ball. The movement of the wrists in this direction should be concurrent with the more horizontally directed wrist snap that you normally use on a topspin ground stroke, but the total amount of wrist action will far exceed it. Here's how it's done: Open the racquet face slightly as you

The excessively topspun shot, hit in this case with a loop backswing

1. From the ready position, the shoulders are turned and the racquet goes back with the head elevated above the hands.

2. At the completion of the takeaway, the racquet head is at the height of the head.

3. The racquet begins its descent down to a point where it will approach the ball from well below. The wrists are laid back. The stance is closed.

4. The wrists are snapped forward and upward as the racquet continues its low approach to contact.

3.   4.

7.   8.

5. Here you see the perpendicular racquet head brushing up the back of the ball to impart heavy topspin as the hips and shoulders begin to rotate.

6. The head proceeds abruptly up and through after contact as the face has turned over a bit.

7. The elbows bend in unison as the racquet is taken into the high follow-through position slightly beyond the shoulder.

8. For maximum topspin as on the moonball or topspin lob, the follow-through can be even longer, passing even farther beyond the shoulder and down the back. This length is the natural result of a very abrupt upward/vertical stroke. The weight transfer on this shot is as much upward as forward.

Catherine Tanvier is the most adept among the women pros at turning the face over the ball to produce excessive topspin.

are approaching the ball, closing it to the "perfect perpendicular" by snapping your wrists *forward, upward, and over* in a clockwise direction for either the right-handed, two-handed backhand, or the left-handed, two-handed forehand, and in a counterclockwise direction for either the right-handed, two-handed forehand, or the left-handed, two-handed backhand. Notice that at a point approximately halfway between the point of contact and the finish, the racquet face has turned downward toward the court.

As the racquet face quickly passes over the ball, you must try to allow it to roll down and contact as many strings as possible. The more the better—give it the superbrush! Remember to be patient with yourself though, as this shot requires superb timing, and with so little room for error, it may be some time before you fully acquire the knack for it. And beware of falling into the trap of trying to turn the face over the ball too much on other shots requiring less topspin, unless, of course, you're blessed with those magical Swedish wrists. (It should be noted, here, that Jimmy Connors also has a great backhand topspin lob, which he hits with little or no wrist action, proving that you don't have to snap your wrists forward or turn the face over to create a lot of topspin, though it sure helps!)

The Significance of the Topspin Lob in the Two-Handed Style

A special word should be offered regarding the two-hander's capacity to further confuse and unnerve opponents with this exciting, spectacular shot with which they are potentially so adept. Combined with the deceptive, wristy passing shots, they comprise a formidable cluster of weapons to be employed against a net-rushing opponent (or opponents, in doubles). After he or she has once been "burned" by the offensive lob, an opponent will be hesitant to close in too closely to the net for fear of being victimized again. But if your opponent hangs back behind the proper volleying position—four or five feet from the net—you'll have a lot more room to squeeze those looping passing shots through. With a wristier two-handed topspin style, it becomes virtually impossible for the opponent to anticipate which shot is coming. Will you attempt to pass down the line or suddenly change your mind, and with your wrists, flick the ball cross-court, or will you cleverly flip a topspin lob over his or her head? The ability to exercise such deception is truly invaluable. Your frustrated opponent(s) will continually experience great difficulty being in the proverbial right place at the right time. I strongly urge each and every one of you to work hard to perfect the topspin lob. Although it is not your highest percentage alternative, as a two-hander you'll make it a surprising number of times. So let your opponents know early on in the match that you're fully capable of winning points with it the way Borg, Connors, and Mayer do. Even if you miss a few, it's going to give the other guy something more to worry about, and that in itself will be worth a couple of passing shots down the line in the next set. Let the good times roll!

CHAPTER NINE

THE TWO-HANDED SLICE GROUND STROKES

In addition to the flat and topspin shots, there is another major type of shot which, although it has been mentioned, has not been discussed in detail. The slice shot is also commonly referred to as either a backspin shot or an underspin shot. Underspin is created by hitting down and through the ball, allowing the strings to pass down the ball, as it rolls up the strings. As the ball leaves the racquet, it will be spinning toward you and away from your opponent. Underspin is the opposite of topspin.

A LESS AGGRESSIVE SHOT

The slice is, by nature, a somewhat less aggressive shot than either the topspin or flat shot because it normally lacks their greater pace. It is difficult to hit the underspin shot as hard because this rotation forces the ball to rise and carry farther as it proceeds toward the opponent's baseline. To hit the shot aggressively then, it must, like the flat shot, pass dangerously close to the top of the net, or, if you attempt to avoid the net by hitting it higher, the backspin is likely to cause it to sail long if it contains very much pace at all. With its decreased margin for error, the slice must often be hit with diminished force if it is to be kept within the court. Consequently, when the opponent is at the baseline, he or she will be able to run it down more easily and intercept this slower moving shot more frequently when at the net. Furthermore, when using the slice, it is much more difficult to hit a high-paced ball at the net-rusher's feet because it tends to rise, rather than drop. A relatively hard hit slice shot will usually reach the net person at a point above rather than below net level. Naturally, this permits your opponent to hit a more forcing volley, the higher the point at which it is played. Likewise, it is also more difficult to execute the highly angled passing shot when employing slice, due to its tendency to rise and then sail wide if it contains much pace. Clearly, the slice has considerably less to offer an aggressive player than a topspin shot. Understandably then, there are no professional two-handed players who hit the majority of their two-handed shots with backspin. To do so would certainly be a total waste of the aggressive topspin potential that is truly the *raison d'être* of the two-handed style. However, most of them are quite capable of hitting the slice shot, and when used at the appropriate time, it is a shot that no tennis player can really afford to be without. It can be utilized in several specific ways.

Slicing to Confuse the Opponent

Underspin can be used during a baseline rally in order to disturb or confuse your opponent. Any time that you give an opponent a type of shot that varies markedly from those he or she has been receiving, it may be disruptive to concentration, adversely affect stroke production, and perhaps result in an unforced error. Assuming that you have been hitting either topspin or flatter shots, an occasional underspin shot can throw your opponent off stride because the ball will move through the air more slowly and it will usually skid slightly and bounce lower. Or, you may force your opponent to err simply because the sliced ball will react differently than a topspin ball when it contacts the opponent's strings. For instance, if the opponent attempts to apply topspin to your heavily underspun shot, this will accentuate the ball's forward rotation, possibly propelling it downward into the net.

The "Steady" Slice Shot

A sliced shot, or a series of slice shots, may also be used to simply "keep the ball in play." In other words, a less aggressive player, a counterpuncher, let us say, may choose to slice the ball just to prolong the point. He or she is merely attempting to "outsteady" an opponent, giving him or her the opportunity to err first.

Bjorn Borg used the two-handed slice backhand when he first began playing tennis, but gave it up in favor of the topspin shot. In the last several years, however, he has succeeded in mastering the slice and now actually hits more underspin shots than any other major two-hander besides Jimmy Connors. This addition to his game gives Bjorn heightened versatility and therefore extra effectiveness from the baseline. He has used the slice very successfully in his matches with Connors over the last couple of years. Typically, he has used it defensively, just trying to "keep it going" until Jimmy made an error. This has been a central part of Borg's strategy against his more aggressive and slightly more error-prone archrival, particularly on slower court surfaces. Its effectiveness is now well documented.

On the women's side, 1982 Women's Tennis Association Rookie

1982 WTA rookie of the year, Bonnie Gadusek, doing what she does so well—slicing.

of the Year, Bonnie Gadusek, is far and away the most proficient and prolific underspin artist. Most of her two-handed peers would do well to emulate her by slicing a little more for the sake of diversity.

THE SLICE APPROACH SHOT

The underspin shot is an excellent choice for an approach shot because its diminished pace gives you ample time in which to move forward into the proper volleying position. On the other hand, a ball with more pace may reach the opponent before you reach the net position, thus prohibiting you from moving in far enough to completely cover the angles. Furthermore, because the slice shot tends to rise through the air, it normally tends to land closer to the opponent's baseline, giving him or her a more difficult passing shot. And lastly, the skid and lower bounce also add to the difficulty of the opponent's shot.

Borg's wrists are nice and tight and the face of his racquet is open as he prepares to "mix it up" a bit with some underspin.

HITTING THE SLICE SHOT

The photo sequence of the slice shot shows the author hitting the two-handed slice backhand from the closed stance. The technique for the two-handed forehand is, as always, the same. The stroke is also the same whether used at the baseline or in the midcourt area as an approach shot.

The Backswing and the Role of the Wrists

The racquet should be taken back with a full shoulder turn to a point slightly *above* the anticipated point of contact. This higher backswing permits the racquet head to move along a slighty downward path, rather than upward, through the hitting area. It is very important to realize that it is the distinctively downward path of the racquet head that imparts underspin to the shot. To facilitate this, the muscles in the wrists should remain quite tight so that they're "cocked-up" (positioned above the hands) on the backswing, just as they were in the ready position, to insure that you approach the ball from above.

1.

2.

5.

6.

3.   4.

The slice shot, hit as always with the straight-up backswing

1. From the ready position the racquet is taken straight up to a position above the anticipated point of contact.

2. At the completion of the takeaway, the racquet head is at about the height of the head, the wrists are firm, and the racquet face is slightly open. The elbows are bent.

3. The racquet begins its descent down toward the contact point, with the appropriate arm either pushing or pulling. The wrists are still firm and the stance is now closed in order to transfer the weight forward into the shot at impact.

4.The racquet face is still open through impact as the ball ascends the face and leaves with underspin. The face continues to bevel after impact. The arms have straightened out as the hips and shoulders begin to rotate. The wrists are still very firm.

5. After impact, the racquet moves up and outward toward the target as the weight comes forward onto the front foot.

6. Here you see the elongated follow-through that characterizes the slice shot. The arms are quite straight and the elbows are bent only slightly. The racquet is pointing upward to an area just above the target.

Chris's wrists are still firm, though the racquet head has dropped slightly as she slices under her famous two-handed backhand drop shot.

It is essential to keep the wrists cocked up, also, so that the shot is not deprived of the *firmness* and accuracy that typically result from relaxing and then dropping them. Many authorities insist that you should never drop the racquet head below the hands. Actually though, with the strength of the two hands it is really only necessary to keep the wrists from dropping to a point where they become too relaxed. In playing certain shots, if the arms themselves extend downward from a bent trunk and the racquet head is then below the hands, it may sometimes falsely appear that the wrists have been dropped too low when actually they are firm and relatively upright. As you can see in the photo of Evert Lloyd, both her arms and racquet have descended but her racquet is still at a 90 degree angle with respect to the arms, indicating that the wrists are still firm.

Pushing and Pulling to Contact
As you initiate the racquet's forward movement, you will once more

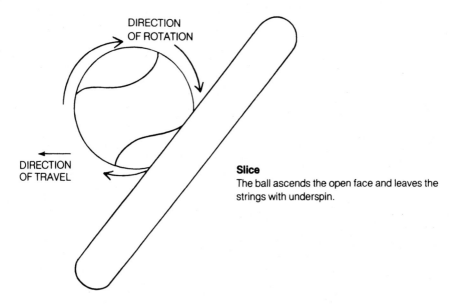

DIRECTION
OF ROTATION

DIRECTION
OF TRAVEL

Slice
The ball ascends the open face and leaves the
strings with underspin.

experience the sensation of both pushing and pulling simultaneously
with the appropriate arm. Like the flat shot, the slice should be contacted a few inches farther in front of the forward foot than a topspin shot to promote the desired elongated horizontal movement as
opposed to a more vertical path.

Ascending the Open Face
As the ball is contacted, it should be permitted to roll up a slightly
open face, as shown in the diagram of the slice stroke. (Recall that on
a topspin shot the ball moves in the opposite direction, down the
strings.) About a 10 degree incline is appropriate for all but the shots
that are well below net level or very deep in the court. If the face is
not at least slightly open, it will be impossible for the ball to ascend
the strings, and underspin cannot be imparted. The greater the number of strings the ball contacts, the more underspin will be generated,
increasing the degree of control you have over the shot. *Remember,
spin equals control in tennis.* Always strive for long contact; the
longer you can keep the ball on your strings, the more accurate your
placement will be.

Turning the Wrists Under
The wrists should "turn under" just slightly during the shot, causing
the racquet face to become progressively more open *after* you make

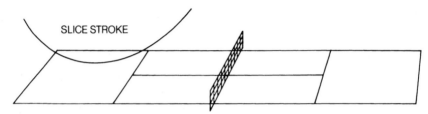

SLICE STROKE

The elongated U-shaped slice stroke

initial contact with the ball. This is sometimes referred to as *beveling* the racquet face. However, it is a misconception to think that in beveling the face the strings actually pass *under* the ball—as so many have contended. In actuality, only on the lowest of shots does this occur; all higher shots are contacted just barely below the halfway point. If you really hit *under* these shots with any force you'd probably score a "home run"—certainly not a feat to make you overly popular with either your partners or opponents.

Think of this beveling as being the exact opposite action of turning the face over the ball for topspin. It is important to realize that, although the wrists turn under by rotating vertically, they should never be permitted to move loosely in a lateral, horizontal dimension as they do on certain topspin shots. Your control of the two-handed slice is greatly enhanced through solidity.

THE HEIGHT OF THE BALL

The lower the ball as you slice through it, the more open the face must be to propel it up and over the net. And the closer you are to the net, the more open the face must also be because the ball must be lofted up quickly to avoid the net. The shape of such strokes will resemble a gentle, long U. When playing a higher ball, one that is chest height or above, you need not open the face as much. When near the net, for instance, the face should be just slightly open and the path of the stroke should be more downward, to drive the ball directly into the court. On the other hand, if you slice the higher ball when in the back court, the face must be progressively more open the farther you are from the net and the stroke will become more horizontal as the ball now has farther to fly. The shape of these strokes will resemble an even longer and more flowing U. See the diagram of the slice stroke and imagine your racquet moving along this basic pattern.

ATP pro Vincent Van Patten is playing the short ball in the midcourt
area with underspin. Notice the
cocked wrists and elevated racquet
head. The elbows will straighten
toward impact.

Now, actually pick up your racquet and swing it, and you will start to
get the feel for the slice.

FLEXING AND STRAIGHTENING THE ELBOWS

Notice that the elbows are slightly bent at the completion of the
backswing. As the racquet approaches the ball, they begin to
straighten in unison, and at impact they are practically straight. This
flexing and straightening is not unlike the action that occurs during
either a karate chop or a baseball swing. In each instance, the elbows
function like levers, greatly increasing the power of the shot.

HIPS, SHOULDERS, AND KNEES

As with all of the various shots we have discussed, the shoulders and
hips must rotate smoothly. The knees are appropriately bent to facil-

itate the weight transfer and adjust to the height of the bounce, while the eyes are on the ball. On a slice shot, though, you will want to "stay down" and lean in more, rather than lift up as much as you would on a topspin shot. Focus your attention on your head; if it does not elevate, you've stayed down.

THE LONG FOLLOW-THROUGH

The proper follow-through on a slice shot is long and fairly high, although a little lower than that for a topspin shot. The arms should be quite straight, bent only slightly at the completion of the shot to encourage the proper elongated pattern of the stroke. After impact, the racquet head should move out away from you toward the follow-through position, traveling along the same line of flight as the ball to increase accuracy of placement. At completion, the racquet should be pointing upward to an area just above the target.

THE SLICE "CHIP" RETURN OF SERVE

The slice shot is especially effective in returning serve because it can be hit quite effectively using little or no backswing. This abbreviated slice shot is know as a *chip*. With more time to prepare for the shot, the chip will generally be utilized less by the two-hander, but there will always be shots that even he or she will have to "reflex" back over the net. For instance, when facing a player with a "booming" first serve, it is advisable to chip the return, applying a small amount of underspin for control. Very little backswing is needed to return balls containing great pace because your shot will automatically leave the racquet with sufficient speed. It is like throwing a ball against a concrete wall—the harder you throw it, the faster it will come back to you. And most importantly, the shorter backswing reduces the likelihood of contacting the high-paced shot late.

It is relatively easy, with practice, to learn to softly chip the two-handed return over the net to the level of the net rusher's feet, if it is hit rather delicately. Or, by elongating the stroke and using the aforementioned full slice shot when you have more time for preparation, you can drive the ball deep into the baseliner's back court with a lot more steam on it. With its economy of motion, the chip is also often the best way to return overhead smashes and volleys.

In the photo sequence the author is seen executing the chip shot. The technique employed is the same as for all slice shots, except in this case, the backswing must be a good deal shorter in order to meet the hard-hit ball out in front, and the follow-through can be a bit shorter also. It is critical when chipping any such ball to keep the wrists very firm to prevent them from yielding under its strong impact. If they give too much, you will certainly lose control of the ball, as well as pace.

THE DROP SHOT

The drop shot is the first cousin of the slice chip. Its intent is very simple—to make the ball land so short in the forecourt that the opponent is unable to run it down before it bounces twice. Sounds neat and simple, right? Unfortunately, it is a most delicate shot that can easily backfire if misplayed or attempted at the wrong time.

Successful execution requires a balance of two-handed touch, disguise, and discretion. If hit too forcefully and deep in the opponent's court, he or she will quickly have you on the defensive with either a forcing approach shot or a counter drop shot. You must acquire the trained touch to loft it just barely beyond the net. This necessitates hitting a lot of fuzzy yellow objects over the course of time, because it takes a lot of time to really acquire some touch. And to prevent your opponent from anticipating the drop shot, you must learn to use the same length backswing as on the chip shot; an even shorter backswing might reveal your intentions. Here again, the two-hander's capacity to take the ball a little later will also help you to disguise the shot. Finally, drop shot only when you are far enough inside your baseline to assure that the ball will remain in the air for a very brief period, to limit the opponent's chances of overtaking it. Naturally, then, the closer you are to the net, the more likely you are to succeed with this ploy. Unless you are playing someone who stands too far behind the baseline or is very slow of foot, use it sparingly as a surprise tactic to catch the unsuspecting unaware.

Here's the way to do it. As you delicately caress the ball on the strings, release your grip pressure slightly to take the pace off your shot. The racquet head will naturally drop a bit as you reduce the pressure on the handle, also serving to soften the shot. (This is the only slice shot that profits from a lack of firmness and a dropped racquet head.) As the head is dropping, open the face liberally to pop the ball up and over with a goodly amount of controlling underspin, which will also force it to die quickly. Try to loft it fairly high to allow the ball to descend at a more acute angle to shorten its forward bounce after landing. The follow-through is normally much shorter

1.

2.

5.

3.   **4.**

The slice chip return of serve, hit as always with an abbreviated straight-up backswing

1. From the ready position the racquet is taken straight up to a position above the anticipated point of contact. The length of this backswing should be a little shorter than that of the full slice shot.

2. At the completion of the takeaway, the racquet head is at about the height of the head; the wrists are firm, and the racquet face is slightly open. The elbows are bent.

3. The racquet begins its descent down toward the contact point, with the appropriate arm either pushing or pulling. The wrists are still firm and the stance is now closed in order to transfer the weight forward into the shot at impact.

4. The racquet face is still open through impact as the ball ascends the face and leaves with underspin. The face continues to bevel after impact. The arms have straightened out as the hips and shoulders begin to rotate. The wrists are still very firm.

5. Here you see the shorter and lower follow-through that characterizes the two-handed slice chip. Compare it to the much longer and higher follow-through of the full slice shot, as shown in the previous photo sequence.

than any other slice shot. Gene Mayer and Chris Evert Lloyd are the top drop-shot artists among the two-handed pros. Chris, with her extraordinary touch and the capacity to completely conceal the shot, attempts more, and wins more points with the drop shot than anyone else in recent memory. As a youth, she perfected this shot on the slow clay courts of Florida, which help to really put the brakes on the ball.

SLICING FROM THE OPEN STANCE

Once again, only after you have learned to slice the ball from the stronger closed stance, should you begin learning to hit this shot from the open stance. Remember, it is often advantageous to return this way due to the quickness with which you can position yourself. There may not be time to step onto your leading foot, anyway, when dealing with one of those big, flat, intimidating first serves that you

Chrissie has no choice but to play this wide ball with underspin from the open stance because her opponent has hit the ball behind her and she does not have time to close her stance and step in.

will all run up against eventually. Chipping from the open stance is often the best way to return against the powerful serve and volleyer.

When rallying from the baseline, however, it is advisable to use the open position less often when slicing than when hitting flat or with topspin. With the decreased pace of underspin, you will sacrifice even more power if you stroke the ball facing the net. There will, of course, be times when you're jammed by a shot and will have no choice but to slice or chip from the open stance; nevertheless, try to step in whenever you can.

HANDLING HIGH BALLS

With the two-handed slice, it becomes rather easy to deal with those balls that bounce to head height or higher. Certainly, many one-handers have a definite exploitable weakness when attempting to

Jimmy Connors will slice down and through this high ball; the racquet face is just beginning to open.

play these shots on their less educated nondominant backhand side. They simply lack the strength either to drive down and through these high bouncers, or to hit up and over them, because they can't get their bodies into the really high ones; on these occasions you kind of have to muscle the ball.

Jimmy Connors usually plays the high backhand with a little bit of underspin. And, as you might expect, he hits it about as well as anyone. In order to slice the high ball, you must be able to reach high enough to place the racquet head above the point of contact. If you cannot reach this high, the shot is probably an overhead smash.

Fortunately, a ball on this level can also be hit flat or with some topspin. Both of the little guys—Harold Solomon and Eddie Dibbs—who must deal with a disproportionate number of high balls, like to jump high off the ground to brush up and over the high bouncer with a closed racquet face to generate some "top." A slightly closed face, as opposed to a perpendicular angle, will prevent

Harold Solomon is leaving the ground to stroke this high bouncer with plenty of topspin.

the high ball from sailing beyond the baseline. Naturally, the face must shift more toward the perpendicular as you stroke balls progressively lower.

THE DEFENSIVE AND OFFENSIVE UNDERSPIN LOBS

There are two final underspin shots that we have yet to mention. The first, the defensive lob, is most often used to drive the opponent back from the net at times when you either are running at full speed and out of position, off balance (here again, in both cases, the strength of two hands comes to the rescue) or are so far behind the baseline that you have little or no chance of scoring with a passing shot. It should be struck with the same basic slice technique used to produce some controlling underspin. In contrast to the conventional slice shot, though, you must lift up as the ball ascends the strings as you also

A stable two-handed flick of the wrists will help Carling Bassett send up a defensive lob so that she may recover her position.

open the face. The more open it becomes through impact, the higher the ball will rise, buying additional time to recover your position. You may also force the opponent either to miss an overhead smash played from deep in the court, or hit it weakly enough to allow you to suddenly recover from the abyss of strategic demise.

The underspin lob can also be lifted up just above the point of the opponent's maximum vertical reach, and if the ball gets beyond him or her quickly enough, it may not be retrievable. However, there is a considerably smaller margin for error when lobbing *offensively* without topspin because you cannot lift the ball up as high above the opponent's point of maximum reach and still bring it down as suddenly. The lower and slower moving underspin offensive lob is more likely to be overtaken and smashed away or else sail long out of court. This shot is normally most effective when used at distances closer to the net to allow it to more quickly get beyond the opponent. The farther you are from the net when you choose this shot, the more time you grant him or her to backpedal and set up for a smash. Jimmy Connors has perhaps the best offensive underspin lob in all of tennis off of his backhand side. With all of his power, it's very easy to overlook the amount of touch he also possesses. And whether attempting to lob defensively—as a last resort—or to score a winner, he always tries to lob *deep*; Jimmy doesn't want to give his opponents any short, easy overheads. If he's going to miss, he's going to go down fighting by missing too long, never too short.

CHAPTER TEN
TWO-HANDED PREPARATION

Preparation can be defined as the movement of the racquet from the ready position to the point at which it contacts the ball. In actuality, there are several forms that the combined phases of backswing (the takeaway toward the fence behind) and acceleration (the forward approach to the ball) may assume. *But the real key to spin, and thus style, is the matter of how high or low the racquet head ascends or descends in its acceleration to impact.*

THE FOUR MAJOR STYLES

There are four distinct types of preparation used by the top two-handers to execute the various two-handed shots we have discussed. They are the straight-back, the loop, the semielliptical, and the straight-up. And again, these techniques have pluses and minuses that you should be aware of in choosing the style of two-handed attack that is the best for you.

Straight-Back
As the name implies, the straight-back technique consists of a simple straight-line movement, downward to the point at which the racquet's forward progress will begin. On its acceleration to contact, it follows nearly the same path as on the takeaway. If the shot is to contain little topspin, the racquet head will *begin* this acceleration from just slightly below the point of contact. In other words, the entire preparation will have taken place on a relatively high overall level. On the other hand, the acceleration to the ball must begin on a good deal lower level if topspin is intended; the entire movement will occur on a relatively low level. And for the topspin shot, the head may actually descend slightly below the level of the hands, as you see Harold Solomon doing here. Solomon's wrists are really dropped, laid back, cocked, and ready to fire! But don't worry—even though he's dropped his racquet head, he won't lose control with that strong two-handed grip.

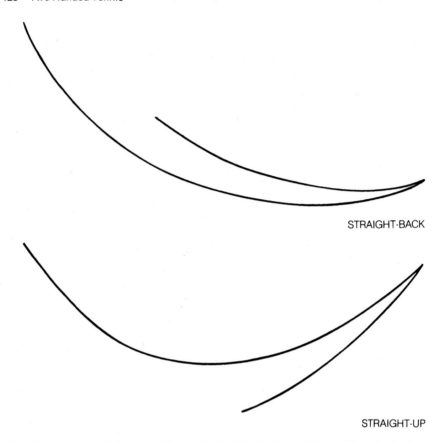

STRAIGHT-BACK

STRAIGHT-UP

The path the racquet head travels on the straight-back backswing and the straight-up backswing.

It is interesting to note that Solomon even drops the racquet head while waiting in the ready position. When I first observed this, I wondered, "What is this guy doing?" But for those who take the racquet straight back and use a good deal of topspin, this unorthodoxy is not a liability. On the contrary, the dropped head eliminates the need to lower it on the backswing, thereby enabling the racquet head to most swiftly complete its journey into the hitting position and then out to the point of contact. I'd like to point out, however, that Solomon rarely if ever slices or chips a backhand, preferring to really attack the ball while applying heavy topspin. If he were a slicer, the dropped head would certainly be a hindrance. Those of you who wisely plan to diversify as much as possible by consolidating the slice into your game should keep the racquet head nice and high in the ready position. You'll find it easier to drop it down, with the

For Harold Solomon the head is dropped, the wrists are cocked, laid back, and set to go!

aid of gravity, when you want some topspin, than to lift it up, fighting the big "G" when you want to slice.

The Loop, or Elliptical, Backswing

With the racquet head up in the ready position, the head is maintained above the wrists as the racquet goes back, and is then dropped to the level of the wrists at the completion of the backswing. The entire racquet is then taken down to varying levels below the contact point, depending on the amount of spin desired. In its journey from the ready position to impact, the racquet has traced the shape of a relatively large oval.

Several well-known competitors use the loop backswing. For instance, Eddie Dibbs uses the loop to dip well below the ball to produce considerable topspin. Cliff Drysdale also favors the loop, but usually doesn't opt for quite as much topspin as Dibbs. An impressive line-up of flatter hitters, including Chris Evert Lloyd, Tracy

Harold Solomon in the ready position. What is this guy doing?

Austin, Frew McMillan, and Bonnie Gadusek, also use loop back-swings of varying sizes.

The Semielliptical Backswing
As the shoulders turn, the racquet is first taken straight back, on a slightly lower plane than the elliptical backswing, but on a slightly higher plane than the straight-back backswing. The racquet is then lifted up above the point of contact. From this position, it then descends again, accelerating to the ball from varying levels below, depending again on the amount of topspin desired. The entire motion of the racquet prior to impact resembles the bottom portion of an oval, or a minielliptical backswing. It is slightly smaller, and hence more compact and less time consuming than the full loop, simply because the takeaway backswing phase is on a lower level relative to the position of the racquet in the ready position.

With this preparation, Bjorn Borg allows his racquet to approach

Gene Mayer is poised at the top of his semielliptical preparation.

the ball from well below to generate the heavy topspin that is partially responsible for making his an international household name. Jimmy Connors also takes his racquet down, up and under again, but of course not so far under. He is perhaps the flattest hitter in all of professional tennis.

There is one other noteworthy difference between the backhand backswings of these great rivals. At the completion of the backswing, Connors's nondominant arm is straighter than Borg's because Jimmy, like most of the flatter hitters, takes the racquet back a little farther. This functions to further accelerate the racquet head while it also augments his tremendous weight transfer. This guy is literally throwing his body at the ball. Is it any wonder that, pound for pound, Connors is the most powerful hitter in tennis? Borg, on the other hand, like most of the other topspinners who favor this preparation, takes the racquet head up more abruptly with the wrists and not as much with the arms, so that the former supply a higher per-

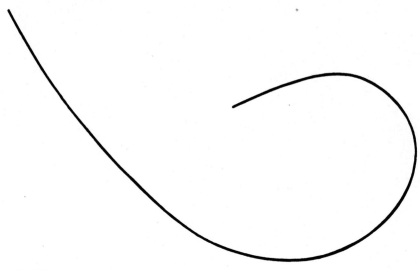

THE LOOP

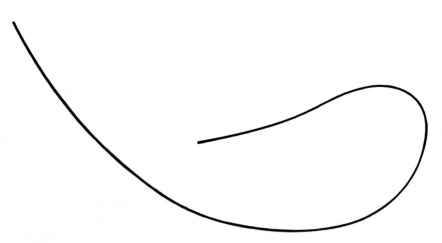

THE SEMIELLIPSE

The path the racquet head travels on the loop backswing and the semielliptical backswing.

The Borg semielliptical backswing. Notice how bent his nondominant arm is.

centage of the overall power on his backhand. In other words, Bjorn doesn't use his shoulders quite as much as Jimmy does. The new Swedish wunderkind, Mats Wilander, uses a semiellipse nearly identical to Bjorn's on his two-handed topspin backhand. However, those who claim that Mats is merely a Borg clone are mistaken. His style is similar but by no means identical. If you compare the two, you will discover that Bjorn normally uses a little more topspin, partly because he lays his wrists back and snaps them a bit more on the backhand, and he also follows through a little higher. Mats seems to have a little more confidence in the down-the-line shot and uses it a little more often than his elder countryman.

Among the top women, Andrea Jaegar uses the semiellipse but doesn't take the racquet up nearly as high as either Connors and Borg, or Gene Mayer, who also favors this type of preparation. Andrea's preparation is actually a little difficult to classify because it's really about halfway between the straight-back and the semiellipse.

The Connors semielliptical
backswing. Notice that
his nondominant arm is
straighter than Borg's as the
racquet is taken back a little
farther.

It's a little bit too high to be a straight-back backswing, so we'll have to classify it as a semiellipse. Andrea, like her friend and rival Tracy Austin, has a lot of variety, alternating between hitting almost flat to moonballing her opponents. The fans are always in for a treat when these two play; they have such tremendous control of their ground strokes that their baseline exchanges seem to go on forever as tension escalates with each succeeding shot. Theirs has been a very tough rivalry, highlighted by some very long and close matches, despite the fact that Tracy holds a decisive 6–1 edge.

How Low Can You Go?
With the two elliptical movements, there is no hard and fast relationship between the one you use and the type of shot that can be produced. As the great players demonstrate, radically differing degrees of topspin can be applied using the same type of preparation. The critical factor is the path of the racquet's forward acceleration to the ball—the lower you go, the more topspin you'll get (remembering, also, that you must combine the low acceleration with a slightly more abrupt stroke and high follow-through).

The Straight-Up Backswing

Most often, slice is applied by simply taking the racquet straight back and up, and then down, outward, and through the ball. This backswing is quite similar to the semiellipse, but is slightly more abrupt and directly upward and not so much of a longer flowing movement. The semiellipse may also be used to apply underspin, but it is a little speedier to go straight up. These closely related movements are the only acceptable preparations to use whenever you want to slice the ball.

WHICH BACKSWING TO USE?

The primary advantage of the straight-back method is its simplicity. It is easier to learn than either of the elliptical movements, allowing its practitioners to groove it most rapidly. It is also less time consuming, which becomes a very important consideration when playing on faster court surfaces or when returning serves or other high-paced shots. This loopless motion is the lowest common denominator in backswings; it grants you the best chance of meeting the hardest hit balls out in front, whereas the slower elliptical movements may cause you to hit these same shots late—at least until you become more adept with the loop. Despite these advantages, only a few world class two-handers—Harold Solomon, Kathy Rinaldi, Andrea Leand, Mary Lou Piatek, and Carling Bassett—take the racquet straight back because it is the least powerful form of preparation.

Certainly, beginners should learn initially to take the racquet straight back. Then, after they can solidly contact the ball, they may begin to experiment with one of the more potent elliptical motions. Although it is more difficult to time the ball with a loop, it is inherently more powerful because the racquet is moving downward with the force of gravity and not upward against it, as with the straight-back backswing. Here is yet another key to Connors's great power.

The semiellipse in particular is also quite versatile because the initial upward movement of the racquet puts Jimmy into the position to slice if he wants to. The great number of underspin shots that he actually hits tend to go unnoticed in the shadow of the greater ferocity of his flat two-hander. His is perhaps the single most effective backhand in tennis today. With this one backswing, Jimmy has all the shots: he can hit flat with practically superhuman consistency, he can hit with more topspin when required—on a passing shot, for instance, he can slice, he can hit both underspin and topspin lobs, and he can score with an occasional drop shot.

Jimmy Connors—ready to slice down and through!

The loop backswing produces the most momentum because the racquet head travels the greatest distance to impact and is also in harmony with gravity. Research done by Vic Braden proves that the racquet actually gains six miles per hour in velocity for every foot it travels during the loop. But beware its size! Even with the two-hander's extra strength that can bring the racquet through the hitting area more quickly, if the loop becomes too large and thus time consuming, it can become a serious impediment. The only thing worse than missing a ball altogether is hitting it late! Notice the size of the best such loop backswings; Evert Lloyd's and Austin's are so compact as to be almost indistinguishable. Indeed, you must look closely, several times, to know for certain if they even have a loop. The extra power of a fuller loop, like the ones used by Eddie Dibbs and Bonnie Gadusek, has more to offer, I believe, to more one-handers. Most two-handers have so much power to begin with that to make a very big loop is really just a form of "overkill."

Andrea Jaegar, with her "perfect preparation," may have the most biomechanically efficient two-handed backhand in tennis.

THE BEST BACKSWING

If I had to pick one backswing as a stylistic model for the majority of two-handed students to emulate, I would cite that of Andrea Jaegar. With a more compact semiellipse than any other major contemporary two-hander, she strikes an excellent balance between both power potential and speed of preparation. In other words, she is not only operating with the force of gravity but will also rarely be forced to hit a ball late. Furthermore, like Connors she also has the versatility to hit flat, topspin, or slice shots with equal ease. Andrea, however, rarely slices the ball. Like many of the other top two-handed women, she could definitely spice up her game and become even more devastating by using underspin as a change of pace during those long baseline rallies.

COMBINING BACKSWINGS

Most highly skillful two-handers are capable of utilizing different backswings selectively. For instance, when returning a powerful first serve, one may opt for the more rapid straight-back movement, and on the very next shot the same player might use one of the elliptical motions to return a much slower moving ground stroke. Cliff Drysdale is one player who can make this exact adjustment. Almost all accomplished players cut down the size of their strokes—and the time for preparation—when facing a lot of pace, particularly on the return of serve.

As is the case with many contrasting techniques in the game, different backswings can be successfully employed in differing circumstances. And if you have the time, the patience, and the athletic ability to completely perfect more than one, your game will be that much more effective for having done so. Remember though, when variously employing multiple backswings, multiple sets of movements are involved, and mastering two or more is surely going to be more difficult than learning but one. So don't attempt to acquire more separate techniques than you are capable of. Always keep in mind the value of simplicity; this is good advice that pertains to every area of tennis stroke production because it is so vital to completely groove those strokes. In making your choice try to be realistic in appraising your learning capacities, your overall athletic ability, and the amount of time you have to devote to the game. If you conclude that, like most mortals, your capacities are somewhat less than boundless, appraise the alternatives and pick the type of preparation that best suits you and really get it down. Regardless of the one you decide to go for, it can take you to the top if properly applied.

CHAPTER ELEVEN

AGGRESSIVE VOLLEYING WITH TWO HANDS

Whenever I think of the two-handed volley, I invariably visualize Jimmy Connors flying across the court, picking the ball out of the air, and slamming it away for a clean winner. The Connors volley is a remarkable shot because he often hits it with a very lengthy backswing and follow-through. It is actually more of a stroke than a "punch."

A punch volley is executed with both a very short backswing and follow-through. It is a standard principle in tennis instruction that all volleys should be played in this manner, and almost every instructional book ever written makes this exact assertion. However, it is just too simplistic to say that every volley must be punched. The fact of the matter is that the best players often do swing at their volleys. In other words, a somewhat slower-moving ball can be played with a longer backswing and follow-through. And of course, the longer the backswing, the more forceful a shot will normally be. Conversely, when volleying balls of greater pace, it is essential to reduce the length of the backswing in order to hit the ball in front, as you must to hit a strong, well-placed shot. Experienced tennis players know instinctively how long a backswing they can take on any given volley. This knowledge is acquired through a lot of trial-and-error experimentation in match play with both the punch and swinging volleys.

TWO HANDS WILL INCREASE YOUR "NET WORTH"

It is really not surprising that Jimmy Connors and all the other two-handed volleyers are able to hit so many powerful swinging volleys. Their greater stroking strength allows the racquet to be taken back into the hitting position and then brought forward to the ball most quickly and forcefully. Regardless of the pace of the oncoming ball, the typical two-hander can normally take a longer backswing and still hit the ball out in front. Remember also, the delayed contact point on a two-handed backhand gives you a fraction of a second

Connors putting away the high, swinging backhand volley.

longer to prepare, too. Or, when forced to reduce the length of the backswing for an extremely high-paced drive, you can take a shorter backswing and still generate tremendous power with both sides of the upper body.

Power, control, and versatility are the cornerstones of the two-handed method. Two-handed volleys are naturally more potent than one-handed volleys of the same or slightly greater length, and the two-hander provides its practitioners with the additional degree of touch and control inherent in all two-handed shots. The versatility is reflected in the fact that you can take a longer backswing to really "crunch" the ball, or abbreviate the length while sacrificing relatively little power.

THE CONTINENTAL GRIP

Whether your style is to volley with two hands on both sides, or with a two-handed backhand and a one-handed forehand—the way most two-handers do—you should, in either case, place your dominant hand into the continental grip position. (See chapter 5 on grips.)

When you are at the net it is very difficult to switch grips when the ball approaches with such tremendous pace—there usually just isn't enough time. Not only is the speed of the shot unbroken by the court, but you are also twice as close to its point of origin and must react to the ball twice as quickly. As you will recall, the advantage of using the continental grip is that it is a neutral position, equidistant between the standard eastern forehand and backhand grips. So, if you are a dual two-handed volleyer you can hit both shots and also handle those occasional wide one-handed forehand and backhand volleys, without having to perform burdensome grip changes. Or, if your volleying style is the more prevalent two-handed backhand and one-handed forehand mode, the continental also eliminates the liability of switching grips.

On the other hand, if you are among the smaller contingent who sport a two-handed forehand and a one-handed backhand volley, you would be best advised to learn to switch to a backhand grip for the latter, despite the greater degree of difficulty in making the quick switch. You would certainly be at a tremendous disadvantage hitting so many one-handed backhands with the weaker continental grip. With practice, however, you will soon learn to make a quick, smooth switch from the continental you employ on the forehand to the backhand grip, because they are so close together. With this less time-consuming proximity, the continental is superior to either forehand grip for this style of play. The difficulty involved in learning to master the transition from continental to backhand is far outweighed by the much greater difficulty in hitting every backhand volley with the weaker continental grip.

DISADVANTAGEOUS ALTERNATIVES

Rather than use the continental for either the dual two-handed or the two-handed backhand styles, what if you chose to place the dominant hand in the eastern forehand grip? With both styles you would, of course, experience no difficulty hitting the two-handed backhand volley because the addition of the nondominant hand would buttress the weaker forehand grip in the same manner that it does on the two-handed backhand ground stroke. However, you would be at quite a disadvantage when forced to hit a one-handed backhand volley with so little of the dominant hand behind the handle. And it is doubtful you could learn to make this more time-consuming switch, from the forehand grip to the backhand, quickly enough to really hit solid and confident shots. Whereas, as you know, there is a much greater chance you could make this switch in time if you used the continental grip. If, on the other hand, you opt to place the dominant hand in the eastern backhand grip, you would, of course, have no difficulty with any backhand volleys, but you would be hampered in hitting both the one-handed and two-handed forehands because the face of the racquet would be too open for most shots. As you can see, the continental grip is the best at the net for these two predominant volleying styles. Now, here's how you can use two hands to increase your "net worth."

THE PUNCH VOLLEY

Despite the versatility of the two-handed volley, there is no doubt that when initially learning to volley, you should begin by simply punching the ball. It must be emphasized that the punch volley is a very compact movement, only two to three feet in total length. By minimizing the length of the backswing and following through, proper volleying techniques are most easily grasped. After acquiring the abbreviated punch volley, you may begin learning the somewhat more challenging swinging volley.

In the photo sequence you see the basic two-handed backhand punch volley. Naturally, the technique is identical to that used to hit the two-handed forehand. The volley, like all shots, originates from the ready position. At the net, however, where the ball normally contains more pace than a ground stroke, the racquet should be held even farther out in front than when at the baseline to more fully insure that you will contact the ball in front where you can most fully control it.

Abbreviated Shoulder Turn
The shoulder turn on a punch volley is naturally a little smaller than that used on a ground stroke. Greater rotation might produce an excessive backswing (depending on the speed of the ball), possibly causing the ball to be hit late—even with the greater strength to accelerate the racquet through the hitting area with both hands.

The contact point on any two-handed volley is even with or just slightly in front of the forward foot. The contact point on the one-handed backhand volley is 6 to 8 inches farther forward toward the net.

FORWARD CONTACT

As with all strokes employing the posterior shoulder, the backhand volley should be contacted even with or just ahead of the front shoulder. Again, the one-handed backhand volley must be met farther forward—6-8 inches in front—generally making for more late hits. How many times you have seen the one-hander completely overpowered at the net by a bullet to the backhand?

The proper amount of forward contact provides adequate power application even with just a short punch because the racquet will have moved a sufficient distance prior to impact. Again, as with the chip return of serve, you're taking the opponent's power and turning it back against her or him, in the manner of the art of judo. Forward contact also insures the greatest degree of control and placement because it's easiest to angle the ball when contacted out in front.

Even more so than on a ground stroke, it is essential to be aggres-

1.

2.

5.

3.   4.

The punch volley

1. From the ready position, a relatively small shoulder turn takes the racquet head back and up above the anticipated point of contact. The backswing is short.

2. The racquet head begins its approach to the ball with the head up and a slightly open face. As on all slice shots, the wrists are very firm. Here you can see that the front foot is just beginning to come forward to close the stance. The elbows are bent and ready to straighten toward impact.

3. Here you see the arms pushing and pulling in unison as the front foot has come forward to close the stance.

4. At impact the face is slightly open to encourage the application of underspin, and the wrists are still very firm. The arms have straightened as the hips and shoulders are rotating through impact.

5. Here you see the brief follow-through of the punch volley. The knees are bent to facilitate the weight transfer which occurs at impact.

sive up at the net. You must force yourself to go out and get the ball rather than let it come to you. Even a two-hander can hit late if he or she is not aggressive. Here's a move you can make that will not only encourage aggressive forward contact but will also enable you to cut off more of your opponent's passing shots. Dart forward in the anticipated direction of his or her passing shot *before* your opponent makes contact with the ball. Good anticipation is based on past knowledge of the opponent's tendencies as well as the cues he or she is giving you during the match; watch the opponent's body and the path of the racquet on its acceleration to determine where the shot is heading, cross-court or down the line. Of, if you see a low backswing and an open face, start backpeddling in preparation for a lob. Good anticipation requires some luck, too. But one thing's for sure, when at the net, you have to move—to the right, the left, or backward; on higher levels of play if you don't move until the ball is hit you won't have a chance to pick off a high-paced passing shot. Rest assured, though, that with experience you'll find yourself guessing right more and more often.

APPLYING UNDERSPIN

The volley is a slice shot, and all volleys should contain some underspin. In order to apply underspin, the racquet must be taken back to a level just above the anticipated contact point, as it is on a slice ground stroke. And the racquet head must remain slightly elevated above the level of the hands. The racquet will then be able to move along the slightly downward path, guaranteeing the application of underspin. As with the ground stroke the racquet face should be slightly open at impact (recall that 10 degrees is usually about right) to allow the ball to ascend the strings. Remember to strive for long contact with the ball for the sake of accuracy.

PUSHING, PULLING, AND FLEXING

As always, remember to push and pull simultaneously with the appropriate arms, again letting the posterior arm and shoulder handle a little more of the total work load. Think forehand! As you approach the contact point, the elbows, which had been slightly bent on the backswing, begin to straighten at the same time and to the same degree. As in the case of the slice ground stroke, this leverlike action is extremely important for the power of the volley.

You can't win five straight Wimble-
dons if you can't volley. Bjorn's
arms are straight, indicating he has
just made contact.

FIRMNESS

Whenever you slice, the wrists must remain relatively inflexible throughout the entire shot to provide the firmness so necessary for control. The greater firmness of the two-handed grip is perhaps even more beneficial at the net, where the ball usually contains more jarring velocity than a ground stroke.

In conjunction with the direction of the punch, the placement of any volley can be altered by merely shifting the position of the wrists. This movement occurs just prior to impact, at which time they must be firmly set into place again. The wrists must be angled inward to hit the ball cross-court, and remain slightly laidback for the down-the-line shot.

1. The wrists may be angled to hit the ball cross-court.
2. The wrists may be slightly laid back to direct the ball down the line.

THE FOLLOW-THROUGH

The follow-through, which is almost as brief as the backswing, must be in the direction of the shot to guarantee accuracy. Again, as on a ground stroke, feel the palm of the hand that is behind the handle move out right toward the hitting area. After completing the shot, quickly resume the ready position to prepare for the next one.

THE LOW VOLLEY

Despite the fact that the low ball must be propelled up and over the net, the racquet must still begin its approach to the ball from just above the point of impact. The racquet will then be moving along the same familiar downward path essential to the application of under-spin. Even though you are hitting downward slightly to the ball, it will go over the net if the face is sufficiently open. As with the slice ground stroke, the closer you are to the net and the lower the ball, the more open the face must become. Just imagine yourself sliding the open racquet face under and through the ball as though you were peeling an orange, and you will have the basic idea. It is important to realize that you must never hit upward, not even on the lowest of volleys. Unfortunately, so many beginners have just this inclination, but topspin and volleys just don't mix! A good deal of slice is required to control the low volley; hold that ball on your strings for as long as possible to really get a "feel" for where it's going to go. A higher volley is much easier to punch accurately because the net is not between the ball and its target, so only a minimal degree of underspin need to be applied, with a much more closed face. By opening the face excessively on the higher volley, you are likely to sail it long or "hang" the ball up in the air, giving your adversary more time to run it down.

BE FIRM AND BEND

Remember, one of the most common errors committed on all slice shots is relaxing the wrists too much. This problem probably occurs more often on low volleys than on any other type of slice shot because many players simply do not bend their knees enough. Consequently, they are forced to drop the racquet head dangerously low just to reach the ball. Unfortunately, this causes their wrist muscles to relax so much that the firmness essential for control is absent. When you really get down to those low ones, however, the racquet will not descend excessively and the wrists will remain taut. Additionally, you'll be better able to apply the extra underspin that low volleys need with the racquet head up. Fortunately, it will always be easier for you to support it down low with two hands on the grip.

Andrea Jaegar is one player whose backhand volley used to suffer from a dropped racquet head. Now, she has learned to firm up those wrists and keep the head up where it should be. Consequently, her overall net play is much improved over earlier years. This is a very striking development in light of the fact that Andrea formerly had the reputation of being positively allergic to the net. Although she still comes in only occasionally, she wins most of the points on which she attacks because she rarely if ever comes in at the wrong time; she's very patient, waiting for a short ball that she can really "tee off" on. Perhaps this new-found aggressive diversity is just the spark needed to propel her even closer to the top of the pile in forthcoming seasons.

Another player, and a very promising player indeed, who has not yet overcome the dropped racquet head syndrome is fifteen-year-old Carling Bassett. Despite her claim to the Canadian junior championship and several impressive clay court wins (including victories over Bunge and Rinaldi), it is unlikely that she will ever win a major championship as long as she continues to rely exclusively on topspin swinging volleys in the forecourt. Until Carling learns to keep that racquet head up and punch the ball with underspin, she will be a player that the top players will only have to worry about on clay. On faster court surfaces where she will need to come in more to win, she is like the proverbial fish out of the water (to say nothing of the semis and the finals).

BE GENTLE WITH THE LOW ONES

You must be quite gentle, but firm, with low volleys. After all, a ball that is below net level cannot be hit too hard because it must travel upward before coming down. If you overhit (apply too much force) it will descend on or near the opponent's back fence instead of on or near the baseline. As illustrated in the diagram, you must generally attempt to place the ball deep, A, or else angle it away, B, to decrease your chances of becoming the victim of a passing shot. A, with its depth, is the higher percentage shot here and should, therefore, be your choice most often. B, on the other hand, is a real demanding touch shot which will require much more time and playing experience to master. I'm not saying not to try it; you should acquire it, but be aware of the fact that you can't perfect it overnight. Ask Frew Mc-Millan: the low-angled volley is a spectacular doubles shot, and his specialty.

Many players dread having to play the low volley: certainly it demands considerable precision. However, if you will follow the preceding guidelines I'm sure that you will be popping them over consistently in the very near future.

THE DROP VOLLEY

There is a very fine line separating the low-angled volley from the drop shot. If the former lands short enough in the court, it too must be classified as a drop volley. At any rate, the intent of the drop volley is exactly that of the aforementioned drop shot, which was described in chapter 9. The techniques are essentially the same as well. Use the same short preparation and at impact allow the grip pressure to lessen and the racquet head to turn under in order to take the pace off the shot as controlling underspin is being applied. Again, the fol-

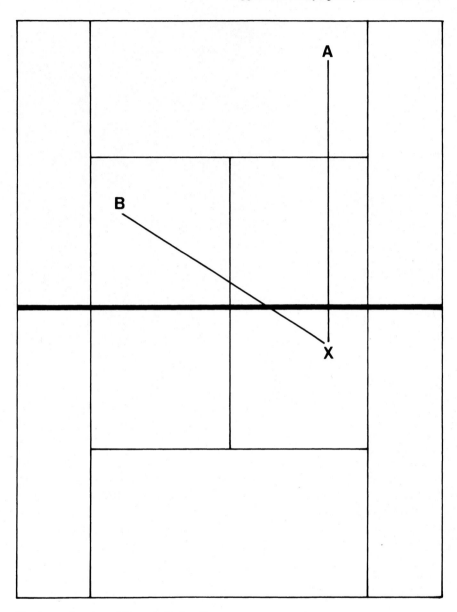

The deep volley, A, and the angled volley, B.

Frew McMillan is really getting
down to this low one.

low-through can be even more abbreviated than is normal to further
reduce the force and flight of the ball. The drop volley is normally a
slightly higher percentage shot than its relative the drop shot, because you are usually closer to the net when attempting the former.
Remember, the closer the better.

TWO-HANDED HALF VOLLEYS

The half volley is played on the short bounce as the ball is just coming up off the court, in the midcourt or forecourt. Like the low volley, it cannot be stroked too forcefully because it also must ascend
quickly before descending. It can, however, be stroked a bit more aggressively than the low volley because a bit of topspin can be added
to bring the ball down safely inside the baseline.

A SHORT STROKE AND A BIT OF TOP

A smaller shoulder turn like that used for a volley, accompanied by a correspondingly short backswing, is sufficient to hit this delicate shot with accuracy. To apply that little bit of topspin that will enable you to hit this very low ball with at least moderate pace, you must bend very low to help approach the ball from beneath. And by elevating from the knees through contact, as on all topspin shots, you will give the ball a little extra "oomph" to clear the net. Unlike the approach shot, though, you should either stop or break your momentum so as not to overhit and lose control of this touch shot by running through it. As always, strive for long contact as you brush the ball. This follow-through is the shortest of all the topspin strokes.

SWINGING VOLLEYS

The two-handed swinging volley shown in the photo sequence contains all of the components of the punch volley. The essential difference is the greater distance the racquet head will traverse during the stroke. The long backswing and follow-through make it virtually identical to the slice ground stroke pictured in chapter 9. Compare it to the shorter punch volley seen in the section on "The Punch Volley." The swinging volley is an exciting crowd-pleasing shot, but don't try to use it when you should be punching an extremely hard hit passing shot. Rather, save it for those shots you can more comfortably handle, or you may end up looking very foolish out there! Even with two hands, you can only hit the ball so late without losing most of your control.

THE BACKHAND OVERHEAD SMASH

The two-handed backhand overhead smash is a derivative of the two-handed swinging volley. In fact, on certain shots that are above head level but not quite at full extension of your arms, these shots will blend together. It is the shot that you must use when at the net to play lobs directed to your backhand side when you don't have enough time to move over into position to hit the conventional one-handed overhead smash. The backhand smash is the most difficult and challenging when played in its pure form with the arms fully extended on a very high ball.

1.

2.

5.

3.   4.

The swinging volley

1. From the ready position, a larger shoulder turn than that used on the punch volley will take the racquet back and up above the anticipated contact point.

2. At the completion of the takeaway, it is clear that the racquet head has been taken farther back than on the punch volley.

3. The racquet head begins its approach to the ball with the head up and a slightly open face. The wrists are very firm. The front foot has come forward to close the stance. The elbows are bent and ready to straighten toward impact.

4. At impact the wrists are firm through the hitting area, while the face has opened to assist in the application of underspin. The arms have straightened as the hips and shoulders are rotating.

5. Here you see the long follow-through of the two-handed swinging volley. The knees are bent to facilitate the weight transfer which occurs at impact.

Peanut Louie demonstrating the
form that rarely causes her to miss
the two-handed backhand smash.

JIMMY AND THE "PEANUT"

When thinking of this spectacular shot, my mind conjures up two
images. Again, one is of Jimmy Connors, this time leaping as high
off the court as his five feet ten inches will take him, driving his shin-
ing steel racquet down and through the ball and blasting it away
from the other guy for a clean winner. The other is of women's professional Maureen "Peanut" Louie, of San Francisco. When she was
a teenager, I used to watch her practice this shot by the hour in the
fading light of "the City's" beautiful Golden Gate Park. I can still
see her jumping high into the air to spike the ball, her black ponytail
bobbing and flipping over her shoulder. She rarely missed!

A TWO-HANDER'S DELIGHT

The backhand smash is another shot on which the two-hander has a clear advantage over the one-hander. Many of the latter lack the strength to put it away because the muscles involved here are relatively underdeveloped, and the shot requires making awkward and unfamiliar movements on the untutored side of the body. The stronger and more controlled two-hander is more likely to produce a winner or force a weak return. The photo sequence and analysis show how it's done.

DRIVING DOWN AND SNAPPING THE WRISTS

You must quickly turn your shoulders, lifting the racquet head up above the ball and powering it down and through, pushing and pulling with a lot of wrist action added for extra power. The racquet face must be closed in order to contact the top of the ball and drive it downward. If the face is too open, you are likely to hit the center of the ball, driving it long. A good wrist snap will also help assure that you contact the top with the face pointing down toward the court. Try to hit this shot flat—with as little spin of any kind as possible— to drive it through the opponent's court as quickly as possible for a winner.

PUT IT AWAY!

You should realize that it is important to put the backhand smash away for a winner because after hitting this shot you will usually be somewhat off balance and unable to immediately recover your position at the net. If it's not a winner, your opponent may then have a good opportunity to easily pass you.

TOUCH AND POWER IN A WHITE CAP

Although Jimmy Connors is better known for his net play and for his two-handed backhand smash in particular, perhaps the best all-around two-handed volleyer in the history of professional tennis is Frew McMillan. Frew is, of course, noted for the fact that he never appears on court without his famous white cap or without his equally well-known dual two-handed shots. One of the primary reasons Frew

1.

2.

5.

6.

3.   **4.**

The backhand overhand smash

1. From the ready position, the shoulders are turned and the racquet head is lifted straight up into the air.

2. The racquet is then dropped down the back as the front foot starts to come forward to close the stance.

3. The wrists are snapped to bring the racquet head up above the ball to drive down and through. I am playing a very high ball here; I'm stretched out to full extension as evidenced by the fact that the arms have straightened.

4. At impact, the wrists continue to propel the racquet down and through the top of the ball as the arms are also pushing and pulling. The face is closed.

5. The shoulders and hips rotate and the weight begins to come forward onto the front as the arms and wrists continue to drive down through the hitting area. ˙

6. Here you see the completion of the sequence with the racquet over on the right side of the body. Notice that the wrists have turned over, indicating that they have been fully utilized on the shot. The weight has come completely forward onto the leading foot to increase the power of the shot.

Top: Frew McMillan has turned his wrists inward to angle the drop volley for a winner.
Bottom: Frew is ready to "rip the racquet out of the opponent's hands."

was once ranked number one in the world in doubles and has won so many major doubles titles is that he is capable of executing those remarkably deft and accurately angled punch volleys by merely setting his wrists to the desired position. In my opinion, his touch and control at the net are unsurpassed. Additionally, he is fully capable of hitting the two-handed swinging volley with enough pace to rip the racquet right out of his opponent's hand. Frew's versatility at the net graphically represents the "net worth" of the two-handed style.

CHAPTER TWELVE
THE BEST OF BOTH WORLDS

The first time I saw Eddie Dibbs play tennis was in 1974 at the Fireman's Fund International Tournament in San Francisco's Cow Palace. At that time he was relatively unknown and his ranking was "nowhere." He had recently graduated as an all-American from the University of Miami and had only been playing on the international circuit for a short time. I noticed that Eddie hit his topspin ground strokes with tremendous velocity and, with the quickness so typical of two-handers, covered the court very well. However, he seemed unwilling to approach the net, apparently due to a lack of confidence in his volleying ability, and his serve was rather weak when compared with those of the other pros in the tournament. Looking back now, perhaps the most interesting feature of Eddie's game was the little curlicue loop backswing he used when preparing to hit his two-handed backhand. It is a very difficult idiosyncracy to describe. If you have ever seen him play, you have undoubtedly noticed it. If you have not seen Eddie play, let me just say that his wind-up is a bit like the motion one would make when turning the starting crank of an old model T Ford.

The next time that I saw Dibbs play was in 1978, in the same tournament, now known as the Transamerican Open. The velocity of his service had increased tremendously; he was even serving aces! And he was also charging the net and volleying winners. His ground strokes had even more pace than before, and his capacity to employ topspin to sharply angle the ball was extraordinary. It was obvious that Eddie Dibbs had matured into a complete tennis player. I was quite amazed at his development, and incidentally, he was then ranked number four in the world!

VERSATILITY

The single most impressive component of the Dibbs style, though, is its versatility. His two-handed backhand, despite the unorthodox preparation, is one of the best in the business. In addition, he is also

Eddie Dibbs playing the "best" wide one-hander in the two-handed game.

capable of hitting one-handed backhands with considerable effectiveness. "Dibbsy," as his peers refer to him, has developed great confidence in this shot because he has consciously worked very hard to perfect it. Consequently, when forced to play extremely wide balls with just one hand, he is normally capable of hitting better shots than any other two-hander in tennis today. True, Eddie's two-hander is a more powerful topspin drive, whereas the one-hander is a less potent slice shot. Nevertheless, his underspin shots are effective because they are typically placed so deep in the opponent's court that he is unable to take the offensive. And with his opponent at the net, Dibbsy is capable of chipping the one-hander at the opponent's shoe tops, or occasionally even hitting a sliced passing shot while stretched out on the run.

THE ESSENTIAL ONE-HANDER

Like Dibbs and all the other great two-handed backhand players we have discussed throughout the course of this book, you too must devote sufficient time and energy to learning to effectively execute the one-handed backhand. Your ability to step out onto the court devoid of any glaring exploitable weaknesses is dependent upon this acquisition. In other words, your capacity to hit the one-handed shot effectively, whenever you come up a little bit short, will nullify any slight restriction in reach of your two-handed shot.

To be specific, I advocate that you concentrate on the one-handed slice backhand rather than the topspin backhand because it is much easier to learn due to the fact that the stroke is flowing downward with the force of gravity, rather than upward against it. As you know, the one-handed topspin backhand is generally much more difficult to acquire because considerable strength is required to hit up and through the ball, particularly when you're stretched out to the max and on the run. Even when comfortably positioned, many people are simply not strong enough to master this nondominant side movement with just one limb. However, everyone possesses the strength to play the one-handed slice, even when fully extended and off balance. It is to the one-handed topspin shot what running downhill is to running uphill—much easier!

THE ONE-HANDED FOREHAND

If you are a two-handed forehand player and must play an extremely wide ball on this side, you should opt for the more aggressive one-handed topspin shot. On this your stronger, dominant side, it is less likely that you will have difficulty hitting upward through the ball, although you may experience some decrement in either topspin, power, or control without the nondominant member.

AN UNFORGETTABLE ONE-HANDER

Believe me, if some day you can clinch a big match with a one-handed shot as Jimmy Connors did against Adrianno Panatta in the 1978 U.S. Open, you will be very glad that you took the time to perfect this shot. In this quarterfinal match, with both players performing at their peak for over three hours, Connors hit one of the greatest

An unforgettable one-hander!

shots which I and many other observers had ever had the thrill of wit-
nessing. With Panatta serving at 5–6 and deuce in the fifth and deciding set, he hit an extremely angled volley to Connors's backhand
side, after having intercepted Connors's down-the-line forehand
passing attempt. Connors was somehow just able to reach the wide
volley, and with a desperate lunge, while running at full tilt and way
out of court, he sliced it down the line, on the line, with one hand,
for a winning placement. The crowd exploded in response to this one
in a million shot! The Italian, never dreaming that Jimmy could even
reach the ball, had not moved an inch after hitting the wide volley.
On the very next point, apparently shocked and stunned, Panatta
double-faulted to give Connors the match. Jimmy had luckily
avoided deciding an uncertain tie-breaker, thanks in good part to a
brilliant and memorable one-handed shot.

HITTING THE ONE-HANDED SLICE

You should have no difficulty acquiring this shot after having first
learned the two-handed slice backhand. The only difference, besides
the obvious absence of the nondominant arm (and it's resulting fore-

1.

2.

5.

6.

3.   **4.**

The one-handed backhand slice, hit in this case with a semielliptical backswing

1. From the ready position, a full shoulder turn takes the racquet straight up above the anticipated point of contact.

2. At the completion of the takeaway, the racquet head is positioned behind the head, and the
right foot has come forward to close the stance.

3. The racquet head is approaching the ball from above with a firm wrist and a slightly open
face. But squeeze hard with the one-hander to resist the shock of impact!

4. The weight has been fully transferred forward at impact as the open face caresses the ball.
Notice that the ball has been contacted a full 12 inches in front of the forward foot as is appropriate for the one-handed backhand.

5. After impact the racquet moves up and outward toward the target as the weight is transferred fully forward onto the front foot.

6. Here you see the elongated follow-through that characterizes all slice ground strokes, be
they one-handed or two-handed. The arm is quite straight; the elbow is very slightly bent. The
racquet is pointing to an area just above the target. Remember that the slice stroke is always
U-shaped.

handness), is that you must start the swing a little earlier to contact the one-hander a little farther out in front. In the photo sequence, notice the great similarity to the two-handed slice in chapter 9 in the section "Hitting the Slice Shot." As usual when slicing, the racquet is taken back up and above the ball and hit with a firm wrist and an elevated racquet head. With the weaker one-handed grip, you must squeeze a little harder to keep the head from falling and give it the stability it needs to resist impact. Allow the face to gradually open more through contact, as you finish with a long, high follow-through.

HITTING THE ONE-HANDED FOREHAND

The photo sequence demonstrates the one-handed topspin forehand. It too is essentially the same as its two-handed counterpart, including, in this case, the position of the contact point, even with or just ahead of the front foot.

One-Handed Volleys

It is also necessary for the two-handed volleyer to learn a one-handed volley. As with the ground strokes, there will be times at the net when you won't be able to reach the widest of shots with two hands. Jimmy Connors certainly prefers to hit his devastating swinging volley; however, when he can't quite reach a backhand two-handed, he has no choice but to let go with the nondominant hand, while shortening the backswing, and volley only with his left arm. Similarly, Frew McMillan is occasionally forced to volley one-handed. And like Jimmy, he sacrifices relatively little because he has also mastered both shots.

Hitting the One-Handed Volley

Once again, we see that the techniques for producing one- and two-handed volleys are virtually identical with the exception of the more forward position of contact on the one-handed backhand. Compare the respective photo sequences. In the case of both the forehand and the backhand, the head is taken back and up to apply underspin, as the wrists remain firm throughout. As with the one-handed ground strokes, exert a little extra pressure on the grip to keep the head from falling, and to stabilize it. Be sure that you also keep the backswing a little shorter on the one-hander to be certain that you have the strength to bring the racquet through in time to contact the ball well out in front, particularly on the backhand.

The Best of the Both Worlds

With the capacity to hit both your two-handed ground strokes as well as your volleys with nearly equal effectiveness using one or two hands, like the top two-handers, you will also have the "best of both worlds." Remember though, your two-handed shot will always be your best bet; rely on it, as you normally can, the vast majority of the time. But don't neglect that one-hander—you'll need it now and then, no matter how hard you hustle and how fast you become. Two-handers with the burning desire to elevate their games to the highest possible level must strive to develop this versatility.

Chris Evert Lloyd has no choice but to go after this wide volley with one hand.

1.

2.

5.

6.

3.   **4.**

The one-handed forehand, hit in this case with the loop backswing

1. From the ready position, the shoulders are turned and the racquet goes back with the head elevated above the hand.
2. At the completion of the takeaway, the racquet head is at the height of the head. The left foot has come forward to close the stance.
3. The racquet begins its descent down to a point where it will approach the ball from well below.
4. At impact the perpendicular racquet face brushes up the back of the ball as the hips and shoulders rotate and the weight comes fully forward onto the front foot.
5. The racquet head proceeds up and outward toward the target.
6. The follow-through is long and high with a moderately bent elbow as the racquet comes to rest just above the nondominant shoulder.

1.   **2.**

The one-handed forehand volley

1. From the ready position, the shoulder turn takes the racquet head back and up above the anticipated point of contact.

2. At the completion of the short takeaway, the front foot has come forward to close the stance, as the elevated racquet head begins its approach to the ball. The wrist is very firm and the racquet face is slightly open. The elbow is bent and will straighten toward impact.

3. At impact the open face will encourage the application of underspin and the wrist is still very firm. The arm has straightened as the hips and shoulders rotate.
4. The follow-through is very brief and the wrist is still laid back at the completion of the punch volley. The knees are bent to facilitate the weight transfer at impact.

1.   2.

The one-handed backhand volley

1. From the ready position, the shoulder turn takes the racquet head back and up above the anticipated point of contact.

2. At the completion of the short takeaway, the elevated racquet head will begin its approach to the ball. The wrist is very firm and the racquet head is slightly open. The elbow is slightly bent and will straighten toward impact.

3. Ready to slice down and through!

4. At impact the open face will assure the application of underspin. The wrist is particularly firm to resist the shock of impact. Squeeze that grip hard on those one-handers! And notice that the ball has been contacted well out in front of the forward foot.

5. The follow-through is very brief and the wrist is still laid back at the completion of the punch volley. The knees are bent to facilitate the weight transfer at impact. The face has beveled more through impact.

3.

4.

5.

THE TWO-HANDED JOURNEY

Those one-handers who are just embarking on the two-handed journey must realize that it takes some time to learn new strokes fully—even those that are the most easily acquired. Here's where the inevitable hard work comes in. And don't be surprised if you perform below your former one-handed standard while learning your new two-handed style. During this realignment process, many who make the transition prefer to gain more confidence in their new shots in and through drilling and practice before unveiling them to the world in competitive matches. That's fine. The main thing is to groove them solidly and completely. Rest assured, however, that you're going to be a vastly improved competitor when you've finally mastered your new strokes and the unique approach to tennis to which they give rise.

In *Two-Handed Tennis* we have attempted to teach a winner's game by providing you with all the possible techniques for hitting the full array of two-handed shots as well as the ways in which they may be combined in match play—and combine them you must if you are to become maximally successful with the two-handed game. Master as many shots and all degrees of both types of spin, and you will be on your way to becoming that complete two-handed tennis player. Good luck, and may your tennis skills and enjoyment of this great game *double*!